Confessions of a Global Negotiator

**A Quick Guide to the 5 Rules
Business Development Professionals
Need to Close Great Deals**

Rebecca,
    Here's to a great
year at WCFIA.
        All the best!
            Nick

N I C K   P S Y H O G E O S

Confessions of a Global Negotiator
by Nick Psyhogeos

1. BUS000000 BUSINESS & ECONOMICS / General
2. BUS047000 BUSINESS & ECONOMICS / Negotiating
3. BUS007010 BUSINESS & ECONOMICS /
Business Communication / Meetings & Presentations

ISBN (Paperback): 978-1-935953-80-7
ISBN (Hard cover): 978-1-935953-81-4

Cover design by Michelle Psyhogeos

Printed in the United States of America

Authority Publishing
11230 Gold Express Dr. #310-413
Gold River, CA 95670
800-877-1097
www.AuthorityPublishing.com

Contents

Introduction

We hear them repeated daily: stick and carrot, risk-reward, good cop/bad cop. Empty and unhelpful idioms. When you strip it down, there is one and only one thing that matters when building consensus—*you*.

Your behavior sets the tone. The words you choose either invite or repel. Your preparation, or lack thereof, determines your progress. Your choice between getting your way and searching for the right result decides the outcome. You see, your behavior is the single most significant and powerful ingredient in persuading others. And the best part is, you are 100% in control of it. Whether you are making a speech, delivering a business plan, or negotiating a deal, you choose between winning and losing.

I am not a psychologist, nor is this a sociological essay about human conduct. I am someone who has observed—with great fascination—the attributes of both winning and losing arguments over a 25-year front-line career as a trial lawyer, business leader, and most recently as president of Microsoft Corporation's patent subsidiary. While I've litigated cases, negotiated settlements, and done deals with hundreds of companies all across the globe, I can't say these are attributes that I have fully embraced or mastered. Rather, this is a book on what I've mostly seen and admired in others; it's a playbook, of sorts, of winning advocacy.

In 1986, Mark McCormack published his groundbreaking work, *What They Don't Teach You at Harvard Business School*. As with business acumen, the art of persuasion and negotiating isn't something you'll learn in college. Nor will it be taught (well or at all) by your company. Whether you are just starting out, or are a seasoned pro, it is something to be experienced over a lifetime. My hope is that the experiences I share in this book will give you a giant leap forward on your journey.

About Me

I was born into a somewhat typical immigrant family. Both parents moved from Greece to the US to find opportunities for themselves that were lacking at home. They aspired for their children to lead fuller, more successful lives than their own.

With the move came the sense of family and community common with first-generation households. Our extended family was large, we celebrated holidays with aunts, uncles, and cousins, and we ate, a lot. We also argued. Family get-togethers were a metaphorical contact sport. If you had an observation or shared an opinion, you had better have the stuff to back it up. Because you would get called on it.

So, for me the seeds of debate were sowed at an early age. And they grew from there. I majored in political science (i.e., being opinionated) in college and decided to go to law school to become a trial lawyer. As I think back, my gravitational pull toward understanding the recipe for winning arguments was advanced as a Law Clerk for the Rhode Island Supreme Court. My job was to prepare "bench memos" for the five justices in advance of oral argument. Essentially, this consisted of me picking the winning side based on the parties' legal briefs and my independent research of the issues, and preparing a report with my reasoning. What was eye opening was just how often I was wrong.

I was young, inexperienced, and lacking in the kind of confidence needed to do anything other than apply the strictest legal interpretation possible. I was missing the perspective and nuance that the justices possessed and which they called on routinely to ease the clutch of robotic legal assessments in favor of ones more equitable in nature. I recall speaking with one of the senior justices after they voted following oral argument—a vote that went against my recommended position. I expressed my confusion, reciting the court's prior legal precedents that surely demanded the outcome I prescribed. The justice smiled, called out a few facts that tipped the balance toward a different outcome, and said dispassionately, "Remember, the law is what we say it is."

A purist might dismiss this as cavalier or even intellectually dishonest. Here's what I learned: Judges are people too and carry with them the same vulnerabilities to fairness and reason as everyone else. They also are as apt to fall subject to compelling persuasion as you or me. And if judges—who are confined at least to some degree by the law—are so prone, the rest of us are a blank canvas of possibilities.

I've taken that learning with me while I've advanced in my career, as a litigator and business leader, as I have the fascination with verbal conversion. I've observed some of the most effective trial lawyers who convince and compel without ever raising their voice. I've studied junior personnel who wield more influence with executives than folks several levels their senior. And I've been drawn toward leaders who artfully paint a vision for success and guide others to it.

I'm not a career consultant or academic, and you won't find diagnostic charts for improved negotiations in the pages that follow. There are many books out there that already do a good job with that. My intent with this book was to create something different. I've tried to distill in a little over 150 pages a career of learning on a topic that is relatable and of benefit to virtually every one of us. Persuasion is part of our collective DNA as a society. It's enmeshed in our daily lives—whether you're making the case to your boss for a promotion; pitching a product to your customer; haggling over gives and gets in a deal; or even trying to increase your budget with your significant other. There are concrete steps each one of us can take that will *dramatically* increase our odds of winning over others.

In this book, I outline what I have discovered to be the top five attributes of winning advocacy, along with a checklist of immediately implementable tips for mastering each one, illustrated through anecdotes from my own and observed experiences, and reinforced by some of the best speakers and speeches in history. In a sense, it's my best effort at a letter to my 25-year-old self, just starting out. If even five or six of these tips stick with you, I'll be pleased and believe this will have been a worthwhile read; but, of course, I'm hoping and thinking you'll make use of many more and will be pleased as well.

How to Use This Book

First, let me start by describing what this book is *not*. It is not a step-by-step handbook for negotiations, with sequentially presented tactics for closing a deal. You won't find chapters like the Offer, the Counter Offer, the Counter-Counter Offer, Overcoming the Hard Sell, etc. Other works cover that.

My primary purpose in writing this book was to significantly improve your negotiation outcomes by getting you to embrace a set of behavioral attributes—that are entirely within your control—for influencing the other side. The lessons in this book can be applied well beyond negotiations, really, by anyone in any scenario in which they might find themselves needing to persuade an audience. In these settings, your preparation, your pitch, and your perseverance make all of the difference in the world in determining whether you succeed or fail. It is on this point—the tangible things you can do to demonstrably enhance your persuasiveness and influence—that I share my learnings with you.

What this also means, then, is we are dealing with scenarios where the other side is *persuadable*. There are many situations in which we find ourselves where we would like to state our case in hopes of influencing a different outcome. Tools, like those I present, will only help if the other person can be persuaded. Think of your everyday life. You may prefer to spend half as much on your mobile phone bill or your health insurance co-payment. While you might be able to knock a few dollars off, or downsize to different (read *lesser*) coverage, you simply lack the status or leverage to get them to give you exactly what you want in that situation.

In cases where the other side holds most, if not all, of the leverage and you have little to offer to influence them, they will, at best, be marginally persuadable. Your pursuit in such circumstances of a *win-win* outcome will be mostly futile, so my advice: Don't bother. And if you are the person holding all the leverage, there is little reason to negotiate, so don't. This book is about the more common and near-limitless scenarios—in negotiations and otherwise—where an exchange of value, and therefore, negotiation itself, is possible and necessary for you to secure consensus for your proposal, initiative, or terms in a deal.

How do I know if someone is *persuadable?* I use a form of the below chart, which I call the *Dynamics Grid*. It's rather simple. The more checkmarks under the *No* column, the less persuadable the other side is.

DYNAMICS GRID

QUESTION	YES	NO
Did they initiate?		
Do they have greater interest/urgency than you?		
Do you have considerably better alternatives?		
Do you have leverage and tradable value?		
Are you more likely to walk than them?		
If you did, would they care?		

If you are faced with a situation where the no's stack up convincingly against you, it's likely not worth trying to persuade the other side. If they don't, there is an opportunity to negotiate and influence. If it's important to you, then marshal the lessons I share in this book and go for it.

Chapter 1, *It Starts with You. You Set the Tone,* is the foundation for the behaviors necessary for winning advocacy. It covers the heavy-lifting work required of all of us for the complex task ahead of establishing and selling: (a) our credibility and (b) the elements of a deal worth doing, which are the two must-haves in any negotiated deal.

The chapters that follow describe the remaining behaviors essential for limiting objections to— and vastly expanding the appeal of—your message. To best position yourself for success you must apply each attribute, as they build on one another. Diminishing or discarding one or more will greatly weaken your hand by expanding the surface area for rejection, or needlessly confining your window of influence, or both. I've deliberately limited the list of winning attributes to the five I've discovered to be most essential. Please join me in learning about them and, more importantly, applying them. With that, let's get started!

CONFESSIONS OF A GLOBAL NEGOTIATOR

● **CHAPTER 1:**
It Starts with You. *You* set the tone.

It Starts with You. *You* Set the Tone

"Give me six hours to chop down a tree and I will spend the first four sharpening the axe."
—**Abraham Lincoln**

Several years ago, I had a first meeting with a peer of mine who led patent licensing for a prominent, global company. We met at his offices, and I was there to begin a conversation about doing a patent deal that would involve his company paying royalties to ours for the use of our patents in their products. He listened politely. When I was done framing things, he leaned in a bit and said, "Let me understand. We do a deal where we pay you. Or what?" Translation, or what will you do?

As I searched for a fitting response, I couldn't help but think, what just happened? This was meant

17

to be a first meeting, with light conversation and back-and-forth probing for common goals and interests. Nope. My brief opening invited a blistering return of serve, right out of the gate. Suffice it to say, I had failed to lay the appropriate groundwork, misjudged the likely reception, and allowed the conversation to reach a foundational point of contention—all in the first ten minutes.

Many of us grew up watching *Mr. Rogers' Neighborhood* on PBS. (Hang in there. I promise this will come full circle.) In 1969 the much-beloved Fred Rogers found himself in the unlikeliest of places, testifying before the Senate Subcommittee on Communications seeking $20 million to support funding for a concept that had yet to take shape in the US—national public television broadcasting. The chairperson, Senator John Pastore—whose appearance and demeanor came right out of central casting for the role of the curmudgeon congressman—welcomed him with a dismissive, "Alright, Rogers, you've got the floor."

What happened next was, well, stunning. In less than five minutes, Mr. Rogers—neither a policymaker nor career debater but an educator of children—not only neutralized the hostility but thoroughly won over Pastore. After listening to Mr. Rogers describe his program and his approach to enriching and empowering children, Senator Pastore—to the roaring applause of the gallery—announced:

> *"I'm supposed to be a pretty tough guy, but this is the first time I've had goose bumps for the past two days . . . I think it's wonderful. I think it's wonderful. Looks like you just earned the $20 million."*[1]

What can be learned from this? Plenty. First, I would encourage you to watch the video. Mr. Rogers diffused the tension by discarding his prepared statement and immediately tapping into something all— even a budget-slashing congressman—could relate to: the well-being and development of children. Having set the context, he contrasted the norms of the day— largely consisting of animated programming glorifying violence—with his show, in which he reaches out to every child viewer to help him or her realize they are truly unique.

Whether preparing for a business meeting or testimony before Congress, you must come with a game plan. Significantly, you must anticipate where you are likely to experience resistance and be ready with reasoned counter approaches. Your job in a negotiation is

---

[1]   See www.youtube.com/watch?v=fKy7ljRr0AA.

to put your best foot forward by (1) illustrating why the other party should care about your idea or proposal while (2) minimizing the surface area for them to object. The way you position the opportunity, the tone and words you choose, and your approach to gaining consensus will be *the* critical variables in deciding the outcome. And a good portion of this work must be done *before* you ever hand out a business card or open your mouth. Here are key lessons from both experiences and what I have found to be indispensable tips to ready yourself for the work of persuading others:

Don't wing it. Come PREPARED, for anything

Always consider the dynamics at play. Anticipate the obstacles and develop a plan for overcoming them. You must go into a negotiation or a business proposal assuming the party you need to persuade will be uninterested, unimpressed and uninspired by what you have to sell. Do not make the mistake of believing that what sounds compelling to you will be compelling to others. You may be a great salesperson and polished communicator, but if you fail to tap into that which moves the other side into caring and ultimately acting on your idea, your first effort may be your last.

Here is a checklist of the types of questions to work through in advance of any engagement meant to convince or persuade, something I neglected to do leading up to my "or what" moment. The first set relates to preparation required to solidify your position and the second relates to information essential to understanding that of your opponent.

Your Position:

- What are your objectives?

- What are your must-haves and non-negotiables?

- What is your economic walk-away (or bottom line) position?

- Who are your key stakeholders?

- What is your BATNA (best alternative to a negotiated agreement)?[2]

---

[2] The term BATNA was developed by Roger Fisher and William Ury in their classic book *Getting to Yes*. Your BATNA is what you determine to be your best option if you can't close your desired deal. In a dispute, it could be you litigate or go to mediation to try and settle. It can also mean you don't do a deal at all or turn instead to seek a deal with the next most appealing party. See *Getting to Yes*, Fisher and Ury (1981) at page 102.

Your Opponent's:

- Who are their essential stakeholders and who is/are the decision-maker(s)?

- What are their priorities/interests/motivations?

- Will they care about your issue? If not, how will you make them care?

- What are the dependencies you need to surmount?

- Do you have both a reset and exit plan if things go south?[3]

I was once in a meeting with a colleague who was pitching a business idea to a more senior person. Early on, it was clear he had not put in the preparation to adequately handle what he should have anticipated as ordinary questions about resources, return on investment, and success metrics. In short, the meeting was premature. Rather than try and bluff his way through, my colleague simply pulled the plug. He apologetically noted that he hadn't put in the time to adequately answer the business leader's questions and

---

[3] See Negotiation (Pre) Work Sheet at end of Chapter.

suggested they end the meeting so as not to waste his time. This was the right move, but even more notable was how he managed the follow-up. He said he would prepare a proper business plan over the next thirty days, and if the exec would do him the courtesy, he would reschedule the meeting to engage in the discussion that was understandably expected. The exec agreed. This was an effective reset plan.

Speak at the right altitude

Sometimes the most profound and lasting teaching moments are the most basic and brief. A good example was a comment from a former CFO during a meeting presenter's intro, which was a walkthrough of the agenda. The CFO calmly interrupted the lengthy wind-up, saying, "Please don't tell me what you're going to tell me. Just tell me." A few tips on this:

- **Know your audience.** Especially when dealing with more senior leaders, you should always prepare a twenty-minute, two-minute and twenty-second version, even if you're allotted more time. An organizational-health firm developed a behavioral profiling system called "Project Insights" that I once took with my team. One of the dominant behavioral profiles was of someone *decisive*. The guidance for dealing with such folks was set forth as: *Be Brief, Be Bright, Be Gone.*[4] Practice that.

Indeed, I was reminded of the importance of crafting and owning a pithy message for your creation when I began reading materials on how to market this book. One source insisted that in order to master the message to their audience, authors must write a press release — in three variations —- before they ever complete their book.[5] A one pager, a trimmed down one-paragraph version, and finally a sculpted release reduced to a mere sentence.[6] The author goes on to describe a similar practice required of product managers at Amazon. Before they even get to a go/no-go discussion with execs for a new product or feature, they must crystallize their vision via a press release. He describes the process as follows:

---

[4] See www.gatehousealliance.com.

[5] See *The BookStrapper Guide to Marketing Your Book*, Tucker Max (2014) at page 16.

[6] While still in draft form, I've included samples of a half-page and one-sentence press release for this book at the end of the chapter.

> *"The press release has to address the prospective customer and show how this new product will solve their problem in an exciting way. The press release is edited and tweaked ruthlessly until it delivers on this idea. This forces Amazon employees to focus on exactly what they're selling and why a potential customer would want to purchase it. The key thing to understand here is that they do all of this BEFORE they start to work on the product itself."*[7]

A great approach for us all to consider as we fine-tune our audience messaging.

- **Always tell them something "new."** Don't waste time stating the obvious or imparting nice-to-knows. One of the most common ways to lose an audience in a presentation is to review contextual slides that don't teach or offer insight. Likewise, if the topic is the marketing of a consumer device, net out its differentiating appeal, not a treatise on how it was made.

- **Focus on the big stuff, upfront, with details at the back (if at all).** I've had the good fortune of managing many talented and

---

[7] See *The BookStrapper Guide* at page 16.

enthusiastic employees; often with far greater knowledge and command of their subject matter than me. Related to the prior points, it's important for such folks to restrain their enthusiasm from leading to a "brain dump" that can overwhelm their audience and swamp their pitch. I generally share two suggestions for these employees: (1) speak/write in headlines (you must put a spotlight on your key points) and (2) put your main argument and the 2-3 supporting facts upfront, and save everything else for the Appendix, or below the signature block of your e-mail. Thinking and writing in an executive summary format is not solely of benefit to execs. It appeals to pretty much everyone, especially those lacking similar command of the topic.

- **Don't repeat yourself.** I repeat, don't repeat yourself! Yes, there is virtue in repetition, for example, for leaders to ensure clarity of mission. What I'm talking about is avoid defaulting lazily to the same thing over and over as a crutch. Think Al Gore's "lockbox" or George H.W. Bush's "thousand points of light." When you repeat yourself—without purpose—you come across as nervous, unprepared, and/or arrogant. But what's worse, you are perceived by the listener, like the busy CFO, as wasting their time.

Know or learn their motivations

This is CRITICAL. No one *owes* you an audience. Like my "or what" experience above, if you fail to explain why others should care, they won't.

An intellectual property (IP) deal I was working on was getting bottlenecked by the general counsel (GC) on the other side. We kept returning to debates on legal issues, both significant and esoteric. It was clear the GC was empowered by his CEO to do a deal or not, at his choosing. It was likewise evident that if we kept the deal narrowly contoured around IP, we'd be absent a willing and motivated party. We switched tactics. This company was a partner, so we engaged our sales account team to understand the broader business opportunities between our companies. Our task was to tap into an appealing value exchange, which to date we had failed to do. We learned their CEO was a technologist and was personally drawn toward the emerging fields of robotics and artificial intelligence, areas in which we also were deeply investing. The IP discussion took on a whole new complexion when we integrated these technology areas into the conversation.

Later, I cover the importance of establishing leadership and control over the negotiation. As we will discuss, this does not mean you do all the talking. Quite to the contrary, in order to understand the other side's interests and motivations, you must elicit them. And you do that by asking and listening. Many negotiators are cautious or downright resistant to seeking information—and critical information at that, when talking about business priorities, as we are here—from the other side. Don't be. It's not only effective, but indeed necessary to best position yourself for success.

Here is the kind of message I frequently use to set the context for my requests for greater clarity about the other party's priorities:

A goal of mine in negotiations is to provide a level of transparency, and to seek the same in return, on matters that are critically important to what we both can consider a fair deal.

I have found that the best way to reach that point is for the parties to share, at the outset, their top priorities and objectives for getting a deal done. This includes, for example, our guiding principles, our key business objectives and drivers, and our must-haves or non-negotiables.

Of course, simply listing these items doesn't mean the other side agrees. Our discussions will sort that out. What it does do though is vastly reduce the likelihood for confusion, surprises, and misaligned expectations, which may emerge down the road as significant—and otherwise-avoidable—obstacles to getting a deal done.

Does this sound like a reasonable approach that you can sign up to?

In addition to soliciting these items directly from the other side, you should spend the time necessary to validate, correct, or complement what they've shared with you through other sources. Here are a few quick ways of doing so:

- **Identify and engage your company's *internal* stakeholders/allies** who have connection points with the other side to provide you with a more informed and complete view of the motivations/priorities/non-negotiables of that company. I refer to this as my "Negotiation Tiger Team." It can consist of sales account managers who sell into the account, product teams interested in a fitting partner for a product pilot, or your business development org that sees the long-term benefits of a deeper collaboration with the opposing side. Where those resources exist, don't go it alone. Tap their knowledge and develop a more complete view of desirable benefits. Informing yourself of the broadest possible scope of gives and gets will dramatically enhance your deal value potential.

- **Conduct independent research** to determine their C-level priorities. Failure to study relevant clues and data about the other side is one of the biggest failures I see in negotiation prep. It is an absolute "lay-up" – particularly in today's day and age with limitless access to digitized news sources – and can be a game-changer in deals. If a company is public, track down the past few earnings reports and transcripts of analyst calls. Look online for CEO, CFO, and CMO interviews, speeches, and presentations. You will educate yourself on recent partnerships and acquisitions, new R&D focus and product strategies, as well as plans for geographic expansion. There is a gold-mine of information out there. But you need to want to mine for it.

- **Develop an engagement strategy** that connects the dots between and among your internal allies and the key stakeholders and decision-makers on the opposing end, being sure to use everything you've learned in your preparation.

Informing yourself about their wants and needs, and doing it well, will send a signal to the other side that you have done your homework, are serious about the engagement, and are prepared to bring value and creativity to the table. It also puts you on track for expanding and optimizing deal value for your company.

Know or learn their weaknesses or areas of need

The flip side of knowing their motivations is learning their needs or weaknesses. The ideas and suggestions in this book are not about soft-pedaling your position to get others to like you or advancing a watered-down proposal. As discussed later, negotiating or communicating from a position of weakness ensures one thing: failure of your proposal. By identifying the other side's Achilles' heel, you strengthen your hand

and give your side the best opportunity for hitting or exceeding your deal goals.

I was the exec sponsor of Microsoft's OEM business in China for a few years. My main goal was to expand business opportunities with the PC makers in that market. A key part of this was increasing PC shipments with a genuine version of Windows pre-installed. China presented unique challenges, combining a massive and growing PC market with an entrenched market acceptance of software piracy. Our OEM partners pre-installed non-trivial numbers of their PCs with so-called *free* operating systems, like FreeDOS or Linux, only to see them get re-installed with counterfeit versions of Windows by downstream retailers.

When raising this practice with OEMs, they replied that any such misbehavior was not their fault but rather was done by resellers operating beyond their control. Instead of persisting with a debate we had lost many times before, we pursued a different route. We dug deeper into the channel dynamics with an eye toward better understanding their implications for OEMs *and their consumers*. Specifically, we knew based on prior investigations that counterfeit software, including counterfeit Windows, carried with it high malware-infection rates. What we were finding was that hackers were injecting counterfeit software with malware that enabled them to remotely steal information from the devices on which they were installed.

With this backdrop, we decided to conduct a wide-ranging set of test purchases of PCs with counterfeit Windows from retailers in numerous cities in China. The results confirmed prior findings that the vast majority of the counterfeit software was compromised by malware,[8] through which hackers, for example, were tracking keystrokes of the consumers who bought the PCs, thereby stealing their passwords and credit card information. It also allowed the hackers to remotely access video cameras and microphones from the consumers' PCs to record conversations and secure still and video footage of the interiors of homes and offices.

When we shared these findings with OEMs, it significantly changed the conversation. Customers of their branded PCs were now facing serious security threats through counterfeits. This not only caught the attention of our OEMs, it allowed us to restart

---

[8] The campaign was called "Keep it Real."
See www.computerworld.com/article/2493787/ malware-vulnerabilities/microsoft--most-pcs-running-pirated-windows-in-china-have-security-issues.html.

the dialogue about our joint accountabilities and opportunities for protecting consumers, and the best approaches for doing so. By finding an Achilles' heel, we not only made the topic and our proposal relevant in the minds of our audience; we motivated them to act on it.

Finding and properly using weakness or an Achilles' heel of your opponent is value creation at its finest. It's not unseemly, and you can be sure your adversary is searching for similar vulnerabilities in your position. Consider these brief illustrations. In a real estate transaction, you might be looking to hire a realtor as your listing broker for the sale of your home. There are two competing brokers who list virtually all of the homes in your extended neighborhood. Within the first ten minutes of meeting one of the brokers it is clear he is motivated perhaps more than anything by not losing the listing to the other broker. It is entirely within reason – and frankly rational – for you to test and, yes, exploit that fact. The presence of the other broker lurking in the background may serve as the eager broker's Achilles' heel, and may lead to his acceptance of a reduced commission from 6% to 4% and the term of the exclusive listing cut from six to three months. Your priorities in the transaction – securing top value and a speedy sale – have been maximized by knowing and using the competitive landscape between the local brokers to your advantage.

Consider another example. You may be working on a corporate deal with a new supplier. You want to establish a fixed price over a five-year term with no minimum volume commitments. They counter with a minimum commitment schedule containing escalating penalties in the event of volume shortfalls. You reach impasse. Your preparation, however, reveals that the supplier is experiencing extreme cash flow pressure. While their cash situation is likely to stabilize by the end of year one, an unanticipated shortfall from a cancelled order puts the supplier's business in distress. So much so that they might consider paying a premium (i.e., willing to consider otherwise non-negotiable concessions) in exchange for more cash up front. Knowing this gives you the opportunity to structure a deal to your liking by front-loading the year-one payment, with savings on the back end and no unit commitment. The making of a good deal and a job well done.

Paint a picture of success, *for the other side*

In negotiations, you will often find yourself in the situation where you need to illustrate and sell positive outcomes *for the other party*. This is particularly true when *you* are pushing the idea. Doing this effectively will be the difference between successfully persuading your audience, like Mr. Rogers, and inviting indifference or disagreement. Knowing your audience's motivations and weaknesses is the first step in getting you there.

About ten years ago, I travelled to Seoul to inform an executive of a large Korean company about changes we were making to a marketing program. The changes, I explained, were needed, in part, because we were not getting sufficient value from the prior iteration. What I did a poor job of explaining was how the new program would still deliver enough benefit to *his company* to make the changes worth their while. He got very quiet, and we experienced a long period of silence. He finally looked up and said, *"Carrots . . .You bring me sticks and I want carrots."* Clearly, my one-way picture of success left my audience underwhelmed. The proposal would have been drastically more appealing had I started with, and focused on, the advantages of the changes to his company.

A popular TV show airing on AMC called *Mad Men* depicted a Madison Avenue advertising firm in the 1950s and '60s. In one episode, the lead character, Don Draper (has there ever been a more perfect name?) was pitching an ad campaign for his client, Kodak, on its circular slide projector. His goal was to convince them to rebrand the product, which Kodak called the "Wheel." Draper delivered his new campaign by showing pictures of his own family from the client's device, speaking about the human craving for nostalgia, which "takes us to a place where we ache to go again." He made his case for the rebrand as follows:

> *"It's not called the Wheel. It's called the Carousel. And it lets us travel the way a child travels—around and around and back home again. To a place where you know you are loved."[9]*

He had them at Carousel.

I contrast this with a pitch made by an advertising firm Microsoft had hired many years ago to help us more effectively sell genuine software in China. It was led by the firm's managing director, who happened to be a Westerner. He was presenting to a group of mostly Chinese Microsoft employees. He started with assumptions about the Chinese consumer, the main one being that their buying behavior was influenced primarily by price. He then shared an

---

[9]   See www.youtube.com/watch?v=suRDUFpsHus.

advertising vision that sought to bridge the price gap between a pirated version of Windows (effectively $0 cost) and genuine Windows (as a reasonably priced critical ingredient of PCs).

Unfortunately for the presenter, his vision hit a brick wall. One of the attendees, a Chinese-born member of our marketing group, with a single statement eviscerated the pitch and, in turn, the campaign. She said the central assumption was false: Chinese consumers are not influenced by price; they are influenced by *perceptions of value*. This set off a chain reaction of remarks by others, largely in line with their colleague's observation and equally penetrating in their criticism. The presenter never recovered.

When building out a picture of success for the other side, be deliberate and pressure-test it with key internal stakeholders close to the issues or audience you are trying to influence. A few guidelines for doing so:

- **Underestimate—at your peril—just how essential selling value to the other side is to successful advocacy.** In other words, as the voluble Joe Biden was once picked up saying on a hot mic, "This is a big [bleeping] deal."

Marketing guru Jeffrey Fox frames this topic in the context of a salesperson leaving a phone message for a potential customer. According to Fox, before doing so the seller must be able to answer three questions:

> *"Why should this customer do business with me?*
>
> *"Why should the customer call back?*
>
> *"Why should the customer listen to me the next time I call."*[10]

Fox goes on to artfully illustrate how to do just that, flipping the focus of the pitch from what the seller does to what the customer wants and needs:

> *"Rainmakers don't sell fasteners or valves or washing machines or double-paned windows or tax audits or irrigation systems or training programs or golf clubs.* **Rainmakers sell money!** *They sell reduced downtime, fewer repairs, better gas mileage, higher deposit interest, increased*

---

[10] See *How to Become a Rainmaker*, Jeffrey Fox (2000) at page 129.

> *output, decreased energy usage, more wheat per acre, more yardage per swing.*"[11]

The same applies in the context of negotiations. Scholars at Harvard Law School's Program on Negotiation refer to this vital element as writing the other side's victory speech. Negotiators who gloss over this step in their preparation do so at their peril.

- **Be specific.** Take the time to construct a thoughtful depiction of benefits to be gained by those whom you've invited into the conversation. I recall a deal discussion in which my opposite was arguing why the balance of deal terms unreasonably favored our company over his. I wasn't breaking through and things stalled. At our next meeting, I asked for his indulgence to allow me to try a straw man pitch on *why to do a deal with us,* a version of which he might consider delivering to his restless business leaders, who were trying to quickly expand their sales from emerging into developed markets. I'm paraphrasing and leaving out key points for confidentiality purposes, but it went something like this:

---

[11] Id.

There is nothing more exciting in business than being part of a company that is growing. Growth brings the kind of opportunities only made possible through global reach. It allows for more hiring, more investment, more R&D, and better products and services. It also brings greater accountability. Embracing the global norms of IP is one such responsibility.

Consider the IP landscape and the examples set by those that are aligning their IP practices with global requirements versus those that are not. Press clippings and legal journals are filled with the repercussions that await companies that try and cut corners. Legal risk includes not only money damages, but product shipments being blocked at the border.

Even more concerning is the long-term reputational harm, which can be halting, if not devastating, to a company on the rise. An IP deal between your company and a marquee IP owner will send a message that your company is serious about its growth; that it will not fall victim by sacrificing the long term for the short term; that it is a sophisticated, global player on IP; and that it is ready to compete in the vital US market.

As this example and the OEM malware example show, you not only have the opportunity to sell value to the other side, you have the ability—and frankly the accountability as a deal maker—to find ways to expand the pie of benefits to be divided among the parties. A critical mistake made by business development professionals is to confine the deal scope to their narrow interests. This is a recipe for failure—for both companies. It shortchanges your own interests by missing out on broader forms of value for your company. And it fails to tap into your opponent's interests, which is the surest way of killing a deal.

Jumping too quickly into a term-by-term negotiation on the merits, without first setting the broader context or benefits to be gained in a deal, is akin to flushing value down the toilet. The "selling" in a deal, like the example I just shared, needs to happen *before* you move to negotiating terms. If you leave the selling until later, it will be heavily discounted if not dismissed altogether. Be upfront, be specific, and be on point.

Business collaboration and deal making are not *zero-sum* engagements

Extending value—even significant value—to the other side does not equate to weakness, or losing. A colleague once commented that:

> "*Good deal people get good deals done. And you aren't close to getting it done until both sides get a little uncomfortable.*"

Deals, like the world, are not always tidy. By definition, they are decidedly imperfect, explained by their consummation by "agreement" of the parties.

Harnessing and delivering relevant and tradable value to your opposite will be necessary in most negotiations; a point you will see emphasized throughout this book. Rarely—if ever—will you find a company that is so desperate or lacking in leverage or restraint that they will succumb to your demands without the need for the exchange of value. The opposite is likewise true: The other side must expect the same demands from you.

In structuring the value exchange, follow these tips:

- **Give value, conditionally.** The trick in creating and preserving optimal value for your side is you should refrain from giving something of value to the other side without gaining something of value to your company in return. In other words, the give should be "conditional." This is illustrated by some through an *"If… then"* construct (*if you do this for me, then I can do this for you*).[12] You may be interested in a longer term for the agreement, while they may want additional marketing support. This may then form the basis for a valuable exchange for both companies.

For sellers, this has been illustrated as follows:

"If you give a sample, get an agreement to test.

"If you give a product demonstration, first get an agreement to buy if the demo proves the product works as claimed.

"If you give a brochure, get an appointment.

"If you give a discount, get more volume.

---

[12] See *We Have a Deal*, Natalie Reynolds (2016) at page 54.

> *"If you give a free drink, get a next dinner.*
>
> *"If you give a favor, get a due bill.*
>
> *"If you give a solution, get paid."*[13]

- **Find the asymmetries in your favor.** You will find that there are often asymmetries in how each side attributes value to deal terms. You shouldn't just happen across them, you should actively and doggedly search for them. What your counterpart might be willing to give up on the cheap, given its nominal value to their company, may be of considerable value to your company. Conditional exchanges can be a powerful tool for smoothing out the economic terms of a deal for both sides and in securing significant value for your company, particularly where the value asymmetries tip decidedly in your favor.

  You might be involved in a patent licensing deal in which you are seeking royalties from the other side. While they might be interested in taking a license, they are reluctant to "overpay" in royalties to avoid setting

---

[13] See *How to Become a Rainmaker* at page 103.

a precedent that might be exploited by future patent suitors. Early on in the negotiation, though, you learn that they are a young, emerging technology company in dire need of accumulating a patent portfolio to fend off patent holders seeking compensation from them, much like your company. In fact, they share with you the specific patents from your portfolio that will best serve them in defending against others. As it turns out those are patents for which you have a healthy surplus and can easily part with a few dozen, or even a few hundred. The deal then takes on a new life as you have greater flexibility to consider the overall economics of a licensing deal when combined with a sale of patents, and they are prepared to pay top dollar to buy your patents. An asset – here, the desired patents – that has nominal independent value to your company, and therefore costs you little to concede, ends up forming the basis for an economic package that will register at the high end of your deal target.

The key to uncovering such asymmetries? You have to probe. Your preparation doesn't end when then the negotiation starts. Your ability to maximize value in the deal depends on the value of the information you learned prior to the negotiation, and that which you learn from your counterpart during the negotiation. You will be pleasantly surprised at how open most negotiators will be to sharing information, especially when you set the tone by sharing your interests and ideas for expanding the value proposition for both sides. The concept of **reciprocity** runs deep in our emotional make-up as individuals. You should look to cultivate and promote that human tendency in your negotiations.

- **Be creative. Define deal value broadly, for both parties.** You should also keep top of mind that there are multiple forms of currency in a deal, which should aid you when defining and selling value both for your company and theirs. Cash is one. But business value—meaning non-cash benefits that accrue more broadly to a company and the priorities of its executives—is another. Indeed, perceptions of your effectiveness likely will grow within your organization if you are able to think beyond your siloed function or group in securing expansive value that serves the broader corporate mission. An example of this was a trade-off we decided to make in our patent licensing deals whereby we secured commitments from Android phone makers to pre-install Microsoft applications (Word, Excel, PowerPoint, Outlook, etc.) in exchange for partial offsets against cash royalties to be paid to us by the company licensing our patents.[14]

Engage stakeholders across your company and you will quickly learn of comparable non-cash business benefits highly-valued by your execs or the other side in a negotiation. In one of my early roles I was involved in building out a program whereby we delivered software asset management (SAM) services to mid- to large-sized companies to help them manage their licensing for their internal employee software usage. The benefit to Microsoft was that the customers agreed to remedy any under-payment for Microsoft licenses detected by sample audits conducted as part of the service. The benefits to the customer were that

---

[14] See www.digitaljournal.com/technology/microsoft-s-mission-to-get-its-apps-used-on-android-is-going-well/article/457246 (*Acer will be bundling the full Office suite with an unspecified number of new phones and tablets . . . later this year, another major success for Microsoft*).

the service was free, it helped them comply with their licensing and legal responsibilities, and left them with a best-practices report for effectively managing things going forward. A colleague from China, from whom I solicited feedback on the program at the pilot stage, shared that despite the noted benefits to customers, something was still missing. He said Asian consumers – both in their personal and business lives – place a high value on credentials and awards. This led us to develop an official certification as part of completion of the SAM review, fully adorned with formal language embossed in premium fonts and printed on thick, impressive stock paper for framing. In the post-review feedback from our Asian customers, we discovered that the formal certification was rated at or near the top of the list of program benefits by virtually every company we surveyed.

- **Start strong.** Baseball statisticians have studied the advantage a major-league pitcher has when he throws a strike versus a ball with the first pitch.[15] They have determined that a hit-

---

[15] See www.hardballtimes.com/the-importance-of-strike-one-part-two/

ter's batting average drops nearly twenty percentage points (from .280 to .261) in that at bat with a first-pitch strike. The same rules apply for advocacy. Consider Mr. Rogers dispensing with his prepared remarks, stating that he trusted the chairman would read them, preferring to speak directly to him from the heart. At that moment, he owned the stage.

Microsoft President and Chief Legal Officer Brad Smith reportedly used a single slide with five words on it as part of his presentation to Bill Gates and Steve Ballmer when he was asked to interview for the role of general counsel in 2002, being vacated by long-time Microsoft lawyer Bill Neukom. This happened to be around the time of escalating antitrust actions against Microsoft across the globe. Smith's presentation said plainly, "It's time to make peace." Smith got the job and his slide set in motion a strategy that led Microsoft out of some of the darkest hours in its history.

Gerry Spence is a renowned trial lawyer, believed by some to be among the very best modern-day litigators. Observe how he began a closing argument in which he focused solely on the jurors' duty under oath:

> *"They [government] have to prove this case to you beyond a reasonable doubt . . . They must dispel those doubts. Not one of them. Not two of them. Not seventeen of them. But the raft of doubts that you have heard in this case have to somehow disappear unanimously in the minds of every one of you"*. . . .

> *"Each one of you have the power individually to say no if one single doubt remains in your mind. You have the right, and the responsibility and the duty to have the courage to say no."*[16]

Consider what must have been swirling in the minds of the jurors after hearing this at the beginning of the closing. Words like *responsibility* and *duty* and *courage* aimed at their heart and conscience, coupled with words like *unanimously* and *one single doubt* aimed at the mind. He likely won their undivided attention but more so left them with seared imagery of their weighty civic duty that stayed with them throughout their deliberations.

---

[16] See www.youtube.com/watch?v=e-Reemd6FzM.

The rise of high-flying – and exorbitantly valued – tech start-ups and the private equity firms that fund them has ushered in a series of reality TV programs tht showcase the sales pitches of entrepreneurs to would-be investors. Much like a lawyer before a panel of judges, rarely does the presenter have more than ninety seconds to make their case before the floodgates of questions burst open. If you aim to persuade your audience and influence them to act on your idea, I would encourage you to study and learn valuable lessons from exercises like these.

I recently viewed one such pitch involving a college student selling value and promise in her newly-created business – called Travel-Blender – as part of a university competition. Here was her pitch:

> "Two-thirds of adults think that traveling would be a fun way to make friends. Yet no major travel provider addresses the social aspect of traveling. Not Orbitz, not Expedia, not Travelocity. Travel-Blender does. It's like Match.com for travelers. Register online for free. Tell us about yourself, your ideal travel partners, and where you want to go. Then our unique matching software generates

the perfect blend of travel partners. And our travel experts create unforgettable custom trips. Our revenue comes from commissions on trip sales.[17]

A short, tight, and compelling presentation. The student not only won first prize but has since launched and cultivated a growing online business.

As I noted earlier, failure to "sell" your position—or the value proposition for the other side—at the beginning of an engagement will only diminish, if not entirely foreclose, your ability to do so later. As the examples above illustrate, start fast and with your best and most convincing points. As the busy CFO taught us, it may be your one and only chance to do so.

---

[17] University of Dayton Business Plan Competition Elevator Pitch, Genevieve Catalano (2012)
See www.youtube.com/watch?v=r_Dgsf4iiZg.

Expand the value pie. Introduce multiple issues and options

Narrowly-tailored deals limit your options. In cases where you have the ability to expand the scope of your deal, look to do so. Single-issue commercial transactions carry with them a high risk of getting boxed in, and leaving you without a deal, or worse yet one that is unsatisfying or regrettable for both parties. The antidote is to seek out and develop multi-issue and multi-option terms whenever possible.

Take, for example, the situation where an author is invited to speak at an event hosted by the largest trade publication in her industry. Her standard fee is $10,000, but the event host has a policy not to exceed $5,000 for any speaker. Trying to bridge that gap proves futile as neither party relents. The event host then introduces a new element. He gauges the author's interest in exploring a marketing promotion of her new book on the trade publication's site, a value to the author that's considerably greater than the $5,000 fee discount. It likewise served as a great trade-off for the host, as the cost of the web promotion was nominal. Expanding the deal from a single-issue services contract to one that included marketing commitments led author and host to a deal well worth doing.

Similarly, a tax consultant and a potential corporate client get stuck on the fee for an enterprise-wide audit. The consultant's fee of $100,000 is countered with a maximum offer of $85,000 by the client. Rather than accept the discount, the consultant proposes three options for the client to consider. The first is his standard price with no discount. The second extends a 15% "incentive" discount (matching the client's offer) if payment is made in full up front, rather than half up front and the remainder due upon project completion. The third is for $85,000 at standard payment terms but with a narrowed project scope, reducing onsite interviews from fourteen to seven days. The client opts for the second offer, quite satisfied with the overall package but in particular that the payment amount was fixed within his stated limits.

As shown, multi-option proposals can be a useful mechanism for breaking stalemates on single-issue terms, most typically price. Don't succumb to a failed negotiation without exploring alternative options for breaking through. And demand similar creativity and effort from your opponent.

Exert influence through control, not power

Absent a dominant bargaining position, and an opposing party whose long-term relationship matters little, there is virtually no opportunity to persuade others through sheer force. In your typical commercial negotiation, your opportunity and job is to influence the other party through persuasion.

While you might not be able to bulldoze with power, you can and should look to influence the other side by assuming control over the negotiation. **How exactly do you do that?**

My answer lies within the answer to one of the most frequently asked questions on negotiations:

Are you better off making the first move, or waiting and countering a first offer from the other side?

My take: Make the first move. In almost all cases, I find it advantageous to move first and seek to take control of the discussion from the very beginning. One of the best ways of influencing others is to lead them through your vision and framework for the deal, from the outset, and to return them to that vision and framework throughout the negotiation. In this context, your framework will consist of the key objectives and components of the deal, as well as a proposed process and schedule for the negotiation, and your agreement template.

By making the first move, I am speaking less about the tactics of who puts the first dollar value on the table, although even then I generally prefer to be the one doing so to "anchor" the discussion on my number, assuming I have sufficient information on which to act (if I don't, I ask questions and learn more to validate my offer).[18] I am referring more to taking accountability for guiding the other side through your conception for the deal and a proposed structure for discussing and ultimately aligning on terms.

Why? Consider what we've discussed in this chapter, alone, about the many ways in which *your* approach will decide success or failure: come prepared, know their motivations, know their weaknesses, paint a picture of success for the other side,

---

[18] Much research has been published validating the benefits of taking the lead in communicating the first monetary offer in a negotiation, as it creates an "anchoring" effect by focusing the discussion, and subsequent counters, around that number. See *We Have a Deal* at page 62.

among others. You simply can't afford to delegate these accountabilities to the other side. It may set in motion a bumpy negotiation that proves difficult, if not impossible, to course-correct as a pride-in-authorship dynamic sets in with the opposing party.

What if *they* take control and insist on moving first? This may well happen at the outset and certainly will occur at some point in the negotiation. Don't panic. Remain composed and return them to your vision and structure for the deal. They may, for example, move first in quickly setting their monetary offer on the table, placing a wildly high number out there. While being sure to acknowledge their initiative in moving things forward, calmly set it aside. Just like you want the benefits of anchoring the economic ·discussion around your number, you need to prevent them from doing the same. It doesn't have to be contentious and should not be dismissive; something along the lines of the following may suffice to reframe the conversation around your vision for the deal:

> *Thanks for sharing your perspective on the economics for a deal. I know you've put some thought into this. What I'd suggest though is we set that number aside for the time being. Candidly, it represents a very different viewpoint on value than what we have for this deal. Rather*

> *than focus on a number, I'd propose that we explore the various standards and methodologies that might be appropriate in setting a range of valuations that we both can get behind.*

> *Does that sound reasonable?*

From there, you should resume your leadership role in exploring objective standards for valuing economic trade-offs and benefits. The pre-work you've done will pay dividends in demonstrating your readiness to lead. Leadership is not automatic. It is earned. And I have found, when you prove your worthiness to lead, others will follow.

Great athletes often talk about the hunger they have to be the one to "take the last shot" to win a game. The work you do in advance of a negotiation should give you the confidence to "take the first shot" on the path to successfully landing your deal.

This chapter begins and ends with the power of preparation. Poor preparation can quickly and irreversibly place you, your ideas, or your proposal in the "or what" category before you experience a single step of forward momentum. As a litigator, it was a standard rule of thumb that you spend approximately two to three hours preparing for every hour of depositions you planned to take. I'm not sure there is a standard time allotment for presentations, business plans, or negotiations, but plan extensively. Get ready, be ready, anticipate roadblocks, set a North Star for yourself and your audience by painting a vision for success, and start strong.

Express Tips Chapter 1: It Starts with You. *You* Set the Tone

✓ Don't wing it. Come PREPARED, for anything. Ask yourself:

Your Position:

- What are your objectives?

- What are your must-haves and non-negotiables?

- What is your economic walk-away (or bottom line) position?

- Who are your key stakeholders?

- What is your BATNA (best alternative to a negotiated agreement)?

Your Opponent's:

- Who are their essential stakeholders and who is/are the decision-maker(s)?

- What are their priorities/interests/ motivations?

- Will they care about your issue? If not, how will you make them care?

- What are the dependencies you need to surmount?

- Do you have both a reset and exit plan if things go south?

✓ Speak at the right altitude.

- Know your audience.

- Always tell them something "new."

- Focus on the big stuff, upfront, with details at the back (if at all).

- Don't repeat yourself.

✓ Know or learn their motivations. Identify:

- Your internal stakeholders/allies who can provide you with a more informed and complete view of the motivations/priorities/non-negotiables of the other side.

- The C-level priorities of the other company.

- An engagement strategy that connects the dots between and among your internal allies and the key stakeholders and decision-makers on the opposing end.

✓ Know or learn their weaknesses or areas of need.

  - Find their Achilles' heel.

✓ Paint a picture of success, *for the other side.*

  - Be specific.

✓ Business collaboration and deal making are not zero-sum engagements.

  - Give value, conditionally.

  - Find the asymmetries in your favor.

  - Be creative. Define deal value broadly, for both parties.

  - Start strong.

✓ Expand the value pie. Introduce multiple issues and options.

✓ Exert influence through control, not power.

  - Take and maintain leadership and control of the negotiation.

  - "Anchor" them on your proposal and vision for the deal.

Negotiation (Pre) Work Sheet

Questions	Answers
1a. *What are your goals/priorities?* 1b. *What are their goals/priorities?*	
2a. *What value/benefit do you have to offer?* 2b. *What value/benefit do they have to offer?*	
3a. *What are your dependencies/weaknesses?* 3b. *What are their dependencies/weaknesses?*	
4a. *Who are your primary and extended stakeholders?* 4b. *Who are their primary and extended stakeholders?*	
5a. *Who is your decision-maker?* 5b. *Who is their decision-maker?*	
6a. *What broader interests/aspirations does your company have in relation to theirs?* 6b. *What broader interests/aspirations does their company have in relation to ours?*	
7a. *What are your non-negotiables (and walk-away line)?* 7b. *What are their non-negotiables?*	
8a. *What are your best alternatives to a deal?* 8b. *What are their best alternatives to a deal?*	

DRAFT Press Release for
Confessions of a Global Negotiator

Half Page:

In today's contentious, hyper-kinetic world, the art of persuasion is under attack. Early-in-career professionals – who text, Snap, and WeChat as their preferred means of communicating – and the more seasoned folks among us who perhaps due to an overly-politicized climate succumb all too easily to the comfort of like-minded opinion, have raised skyward the bar for influencing them, on virtually any topic.

What to do? Don't panic. Don't despair. While the task of persuading others may have grown more challenging, you hold the keys to success.

In *Confessions of a Global Negotiator*, a well-travelled lawyer and business leader puts a spotlight on the critical attributes necessary for influencing your audience and closing great deals in negotiations. Your preparation, your pitch, and your perseverance in a negotiation will be the difference between winning and losing. And the good news is – they are 100% in your control.

One Sentence:

Confessions of a Global Negotiator teaches us that while the art of persuasion has taken a hit in recent years — perhaps due to overly-politicized societal debate and frenzied expectations for on-demand gratification — your ability to win over others and land great deals in negotiations is not only immensely doable, it is entirely within your control through focus and excellence in your preparation, your pitch, and your perseverance.

CONFESSIONS OF A GLOBAL NEGOTIATOR

Chapter 2

Personalize, But Don't Take Personally

"Great minds discuss ideas; average minds discuss events; small minds discuss people."

—**Eleanor Roosevelt**

As a second- or third-year legal associate, I represented a plaintiff in a fraud case. We had sued three defendants, each with lawyers many years my senior. They decided to give me the "sonny boy" treatment, filing multiple motions to dismiss, all at the same time. Insofar as the answer period for each motion was twenty days, they aimed to bury me under an unrelenting avalanche of paperwork, and nearly succeeded. Suffice it to say the firm's after-hours security detail and I became well acquainted over the next three weeks.

I survived, filed my responses (just) in time, and prepared for oral argument with the presiding judge. This wasn't just any hearing or any judge. It was in front of Hiller Zobel, a formidable jurist, author, and law professor, and an anxiety-inducing force for new lawyers. He has since become known for his handling of the notorious British "nanny case," in which Louise Woodward was charged with murder for shaking a young Boston-area couple's child to death while babysitting. In that case, Zobel—considered fiercely independent—vacated the jury's second-degree murder finding, imposing a lesser conviction of manslaughter and releasing her from custody for time served. He was tough, asked piercing questions, and above all loved to "coach" young lawyers in his courtroom. I was a nervous wreck and did what any insecure young attorney does. I pulled an all-nighter the day before the hearing, and if memory serves me, the day before that as well.

Given that defendants' counsel filed the motions, they were called first to present their arguments. One by one, they took their allotted time summarizing their written briefs. For thirty minutes, I listened and took notes as each lawyer had a turn working over my case, every word a Jenga block being pulled from the tower of my legal submissions. With quote marks, underlines, and furrowed brows, I wrote down "baseless," "legally and intellectually void," and "incomprehensible,"—words they used to describe my case, each demanding dismissal as the only lucid remedy. My heart was pounding. This wasn't just an attack on my work. It felt like a direct assault on me and my integrity.

As the final argument was made and my turn to speak finally arrived, I white-knuckled my legal pad now filled with notes and jumped to the podium. "Good morning, your Honor. May it please the court," I blurted out as customary opening remarks.

Judge Zobel stared down at me from his position perched high above counsel's tables. "Counselor, do you wish to proceed?" he asked.

Ready to rip, I said, "I do."

He leaned toward me, lowered his head, and added, "Are you sure?"

Was I sure? I spent the past forty-eight hours perfecting my oral presentation, had to endure thirty minutes of insults, and he's cutting me off? "Yes, your Honor, I am," I replied at once, adding, "Opposing counsel shared quite a bit, and I would like the opportunity to respond."

Judge Zobel reclined back in his leather chair and looked straight up. After a brief pause he asked, "Do you like baseball?"

I didn't like baseball. I LOVED baseball. But who cared? Where was this heading? Confused and distressed, I answered, "Yes, your Honor, I do."

Rocking back and forth, eyes still glued to the ceiling, "OK, do you know how many innings there are in a major-league game?" he continued.

"Yes, nine," I countered, my fluster building.

With that he stopped rocking, fixed his gaze on me, and said—adding emphasis to every word—"You know, counselor, sometimes the home team doesn't want the last at bat."

While not certain, I took this to mean something along the lines of *quit while you're ahead, young buck.* So, I nodded and said, "Thank you, your Honor. I'll sit down now."

Judge Zobel said, "Good," adding he was denying the motions to dismiss from the bench without the need for a written opinion and brought down his gavel, leading the court to recess.

What does this all mean? It means it's business, not personal, so don't allow yourself to take things personally. I know what you're thinking. That sounds simple, but is anything but. And you'd be right. But you must shake it off. When you take things personally, you redirect energy and focus from what's important—getting the job done—toward what's not, namely, proving you're right or getting your way. I was so caught up in making amends for the perceived name-calling from the other side—and perhaps lobbing a few of my own—that I was ready to bypass the strongest factual and legal arguments in favor of the most personally punishing to the other side. Judge Zobel had saved me from myself.

In the book *Negotiation Genius*, the authors describe two failed negotiations as a means of underscoring the tendency for irrationality in human behavior, particularly where one or both sides feel aggrieved. One example involves a dispute between a landlord and its tenants in New York City and was over $909. This was the amount the tenants spent – on their own initiative and without express approval from the landlord – to install window bars in their apartments to improve child safety. The tenants claimed the expenditure was necessary and should be borne by the landlord based on prior incidents in the neighborhood resulting in child injuries. The landlord disagreed. The tenants then took the dispute to court. Six years and the expenditure of over $100,000 in combined legal fees later the matter was finally dropped. Both sides lost. The authors summed up the emotional imbalance that leads to such results as follows:

> *"Not all negotiation errors result from cognitive biases... Emotions can be just as powerful in derailing agreements. Compounding the problem, we human beings are motivated to see ourselves as fairer, kinder, more competent, more generous, more deserving, and more likely to succeed than others. The result of these motivational biases? We tend to make judgments and decisions that are not optimal."*[19]

In this case, a clear understatement to say the least.

Another situation where dug-in emotions and hurt, angered egos sidelined a high-stakes negotiation involved the National Hockey League (NHL) labor dispute in 2004. The dispute led to an owner "lockout" that cancelled play for *the entire season*. Players, coaches, and equipment managers didn't get paid. And owners didn't sell a single ticket or earn a cent

---

[19] See *Negotiation Genius*, Deepak Malhotra and Max Bazerman (2007) at page 126.

from TV contracts. Truly the definition of a lose-lose outcome. This is not to say the parties lacked compelling reasons for their positions. The owners rightly pointed to the dire economic conditions for the teams (nineteen of thirty franchises were losing money). The players thoughtfully countered that the management proposal for a cap on salaries would have resulted in an unfair reversal in salaries for virtually every player in the league (a reduction in the average salary from $1.8 million to $1.3 million) overnight.

While each side got closer to the demands of the other, the NHL Commissioner set a deadline for final resolution. When that deadline was hit without agreement, all league games were cancelled until resolution was finally reached, a full three hundred and ten days later.

What do these examples teach us? That whether we internalize it or not our emotions carry with them the power to guide and misdirect our decisions and actions, particularly when we are confronted with perceived slights, dismissiveness and rejection, or personal contention from others. In my experience it is more often the intangible (discord between the parties), rather than the tangible (failure to make the numbers work), that leads to negotiation roadblocks and failure.

I spend a good portion of the remainder of this book focusing on the behavioral attributes and actions that best position us to manage our own tendencies toward discord and impasse and to overcome those of our opponents. Before doing so though, I wanted to take a moment to share a few tactical options for what the parties in those disputes might have done to break through.

In the case of the landlord and tenant dispute, I think we can readily agree that virtually any option other than the one they chose – burning through $100,000 in legal fees in a fight over $900 – would have been better. The parties could have submitted to voluntary mediation or a single-day binding arbitration with the losing side paying fees and costs. Alternatively, the tenants could have dropped their demand for reimbursement, seeking instead that the landlord donate an equivalent sum to neighborhood child care or community programs. This option could have been positioned more softly as a gesture of goodwill as opposed to a hardened demand for payment. There are many others I'm sure you can quickly come up with as well. The point of all this is to illustrate the depths of irrational human behavior and that the way to avoid reaching them – as we will learn in the pages that follow –- is to first understand that your deals are similarly prone to emotion-driven breakdowns, and second that you stand firmly in control of the behaviors that are both available to you and routinely necessary for preventing such breakdowns from materializing in the first place.

While the NHL conflict presents a less obvious set of options, I share with you one of the more creative proposals I've come across on the topic of resolving sports labor strikes and lockouts. It was developed by Harvard Business School professors James Sebenius and Michael Wheeler and it encourages both sides to the work stoppage to immediately get back to work. But rather than have the revenues from the games (ticket sales, TV royalties, concessions, merchandising, etc.) flow to the owners, with business-as-usual salaries then paid to the players from those revenues, they would all be held in an escrow account pending resolution of the dispute. Most notably, the professors call out a critical requirement that a sizable portion of the revenues be given to charity if agreement is not reached by a certain date to create the right incentive for progress and a deal.[20]

This is the kind of solution that only comes through preparation, hard work, creativity, and above all else a willingness to focus on solving the problem

---

[20]   See *Negotiation Genius* at page 117 and footnote 13.

rather than winning the fight, propping up your ego, or getting your way. In the heat of the battle, this can be hard, but it's what's required. Think back to the earlier tips from Chapter 1 about the need for defining deal value broadly and creatively pursuing multiple issues and options. Your persistence in modeling a creative and problem-solving orientation will, over time, lower the protective shield of your counterpart. And it will foster the kind of discussion needed for breakthrough ideas like the one just mentioned.

Well then, what are the best ways for keeping emotions in check and the deal on track? Whether a one-time or extended engagement, professionalism, credibility, and integrity are your currency in trade. Allowing yourself to be victimized by perceived personal jabs weakens you in each area and sidetracks you from the job at hand: to effectively advance the discussion and persuade your audience. Particularly when involved in a complex negotiation, I have found the following behavioral tips invaluable in minimizing the detours you might otherwise experience along the way to insulating yourself from victim status and gaining consensus.

Move past heated exchanges, *quickly.* No hangover effect

I was once in an annual business review that involved some of our most senior company execs. One of my colleagues was on the receiving end of a vent by one such official concerning an area of our business needing improvement. The feedback got a bit personal, with the reviewer saying, "You have failed" and proceeding to outline the number of things my colleague did not do. The problem was none of those things were within his areas of responsibility. Rather than correct the exec, my colleague responded by saying, "I take the feedback and know we need to turn this around, and you can be sure we're committed to doing just that." When he was done, another business leader at the table who understood our organization a bit better immediately sent my colleague the following instant message: "Very senior response." Be the adult at the table and leave your ego at the door; sometimes—like with Judge Zobel—the best thing to say is very little, or nothing at all.

Set expectations. Establish norms of conduct, *upfront*

Be clear with the other side regarding what they can expect from you and likewise what you'd like to count on from them. You will be spending a lot of time together; you must find common ground in your relationship, and exchanging mutual expectations is a good place to start. (You will see this again in Chapter 5, *Be Accountable and Vulnerable.*)

In negotiations, I always share with my counterpart that a goal of mine is to minimize the otherwise avoidable back and forth caused by clever tactics and gamesmanship. Specifically, I will be transparent about things that I am empowered to decide, as well as things I need to vet with my management, and I ask the same of them. I have found the car-buying experience (the seemingly disempowered salesman incessantly consulting the "manager") does not translate well in commercial deal settings. And there is nothing that destroys credibility faster than someone negotiating a point toward a compromise—claiming empowerment to do so—only to return after landing a concession or two to confess their inability to sell it to their business leaders. This unfortunately is all too common. If you aren't empowered, don't say you are. If you say you are, own up to it.

Another illustration of setting expectations involved an agreement my peer on the other side established early on in our work together. He asked that we both remain vigilant of our team members getting stuck on issues and that the two of us take accountability in limiting dug-in positions, especially on peripheral issues. We agreed that we would step in and decide such things to maintain progress, or at least we would table the issues to be decided between the two of us during a weekly 1-1 sync call we had set up as part of our regular cadence. This approach went a long way in enabling us to close a complex business deal in about six months, less than half the ordinary cycle of a deal of its size and scope.

Related, a rule to live by and agree on early is "no surprises." Of course, unforeseen circumstances or events develop and can't be avoided. I'm referring to those that can. Important developments should be disclosed early, if not immediately. Getting to the homestretch of a negotiation only to share that your fiscal year-end close pushed out your timing plans for a deal will surely impact the other side, and may well jeopardize the engagement, so tell them early unless there are corporate confidences at issue.

Identify guiding principles and "must-haves" for each side

Similar to setting *norms of conduct,* identifying principles and *must-haves* between the parties will help prevent confusion and misjudgments, either of which can place a major tax on a deal, if not sideline it altogether. Clarity and alignment—in as many areas as possible—positively serve human emotion and are your best defense to conflict and personal discord.

If a company you are working with is focused on a deal to better position itself against a competitor, that goal should be surfaced from the outset. Similarly, if you are looking to have your partnership status with the other side acknowledged or rewarded as part of an expanded collaboration, say it. Some deals are about the bottom-line dollars to a given company; to others it might be about PR; yet to others still it may involve reaching new markets. The more transparent each side is about their prevailing objectives, the more effective and efficient they will be in structuring gives and gets, and evaluating critical trade-off decisions; and the better at staving off personal dissent or misalignment.

Of course, *it takes two to tango* as the saying goes. You may ask:

What if the other side fails or refuses to reciprocate?

Doesn't that leave you exposed, or worse, invite and allow the other side to take advantage of you?

These are great questions, and ones I spend nearly an entire chapter on, at Chapter 6: *So, What Do You Do When It Isn't Enough?* Here's what I would say at this stage. Yes, you need to calibrate your level of transparency, in two ways: First, based on what is reasonably necessary for you to adequately convey your expectations in the deal and to paint a picture of success for both sides; and second, based on their level of transparency in response. Similarly, you should never disclose sensitive, confidential, or any other information otherwise inappropriate to share, as I discuss later on. Moreover, you should refrain from conveying your bottom line figure or anything else that will greatly disadvantage your position.

But make no mistake, effective negotiating requires dialogue and disclosure from both sides. And for you to be most effective in your role, you must take accountability to try and convince a reluctant party to share their goals, priorities, preferred norms of conduct, and must-haves. Failure to do so, which likely will curtail your level of transparency in return, will advance the likelihood of late and bad surprises, personal conflict, and conflicting expectations. This is the straightest path to impasse. It also will inhibit your ability to construct a value exchange that will both meet your needs and attract interest from the other side. By pressing for greater transparency early, you stand to uncover additional value in the deal, for both companies.

Let's consider this in the context of an everyday situation. Perhaps you are looking to buy a car. You and the salesperson hit a snag and simply can't bridge the price gap that divides each side's "best" offer. The salesperson can decide to limit the discussion to price, which likely will lead to a walk-away. Or she can start asking questions, e.g.: How important is safety and security (which may bring in to play an "SOS" type service to assist stranded drivers)? How about a new extended warranty plan that covers all maintenance and repair items for the first 50,000 miles? Do you have any family members who will be in the market for a vehicle in the next six months? These questions lead you to share that, in fact, your daughter's vehicle is coming off lease next month and that your wife had read about the SOS program and seemed interested. Each new element provides added value to be considered as part of the deal. The salesperson may have more flexibility to discount in a two-for-one deal, and the SOS service provider, which is a new entrant in the market, is offering a great promotion for first-time customers in order to gain adoption and market share. By asking questions, the salesperson expands the pie. Rather than accept defeat, buyer and seller move toward a handshake on a deal worth far more—to each party—than either expected or intended at the outset.

Keep things professional. Stay focused on ideas, not people

The Eleanor Roosevelt quote at the start of this chapter offers special advice, whether you are doing a 1-1 with your employees or manager, interviewing for a new role, presenting on an initiative, or negotiating a deal. Managers, colleagues, and adversaries I've most admired live by this. They rarely if ever bring distracting baggage into the workplace. Name-dropping, finger pointing, and gossip have no place in a professional setting. If your manager is tough on you, don't spend meetings with your employees airing it out or complaining about it. If a team member is not pulling their weight, don't trash them to others behind the scenes. And if you are dealing with a difficult personality opposite you, don't resort to anger, insults, or personal attacks. It never works. In fact, it almost always makes it worse. Even more so, it creates a perception of you as junior, petty, and incapable.

My wife has great intuition about people and has a knack for aptly sizing things up (like a one-woman focus group). Once, after a particularly tough day at work that involved me locking horns with a difficult colleague, I vented to her about how he wasn't a team player and was hoping for me to fail. My wife let me drone on for a while and finally said, "I don't know. I'm not sure people think about you as much as you think they think about you." Sage advice and very true. Everyone approaches life's situations with their own point of view and personal history that affects how they handle conflict. Don't automatically assume that their behavior has anything at all to do with sabotaging you personally. Get past it quickly and keep it professional. And always keep the discussion moving forward.

Avoid credibility killers

Behaving in a manner that undermines your credibility is the fastest way to personal conflict and the surest path to failed advocacy. Like the earlier example of the negotiator wrongly representing an empowered position that he later reneged on, the following are to be avoided at all costs.

- **Overreaching or grossly overplaying your hand.** Assume the other side is thoughtful and has limits on what they are willing to negotiate, and internalize each side's relative positions of strength. As they say, credibility and trust can take a lifetime to build but can be lost in an instant.

In the movie *The Godfather, Part II,* a corrupt senator seeks to extort a healthy sum from the Corleone family, in exchange for arranging a gaming license for them. Michael Corleone, the leader of the powerful mob family, asks the senator why they should pay more than the fee for the license. The senator laughs at the question and responds that he can charge what he wants because of the damage he can cause to the Corleone business if he doesn't get it. Michael replies:

> *"Senator, you can have my answer now if you'd like. My offer is this. Nothing. Not even the fee for the gaming license, which I would appreciate if you'd put up personally."*[21]

---

[21] See www.youtube.com/watch?v=KjNe9fuqQ8o.

In the end, the senator did just that as he came to learn that he not only overreached, but grossly underestimated the relative leverage advantage held by the dangerous and connected Corleone clan.

I've experienced similar examples of overreach, minus the crime-family drama and muscle, of course. In a case early in my career, I represented Marriott Hotel Brands in a matter in which a guest at one of their properties—a Residence Inn—stopped paying her daily room charge. Not only did she stop paying the rate, but she also hired a lawyer and sought reimbursement for over $100,000 for what they claimed to be overcharges over the past several years in which she lived as a long-term resident. Their theory? That Marriott improperly passed on periodic increases in her room rate based on her reliance on a brochure she received when she first checked in containing the marketing line, *"At Marriott Residence Inn, the Longer You Stay, the Less You Pay."*

In reality and as we explained, the tagline conveyed that the daily room rate would be discounted if the guest booked for, say, thirty days, as opposed to a single night. Of course, it was not meant to convey a guaranty against any future increases, in perpetuity. We worked hard to drive toward a compromise, but the plaintiff never wavered from what we felt any reasonable person would conclude to be an extreme and overreaching position. Given no other choice, we took the case to trial. We won and the judge not only ordered the plaintiff to vacate the hotel, but also entered a judgment in Marriott's favor for all unpaid room charges and costs.

Similarly, I was handling an IP infringement case for Microsoft against a company that was making counterfeit Windows CDs and selling them. They were a modestly sized company, and we had extensive evidence including multiple test buys confirming their pirating activities. Rather than remedy their wrongdoing, the defendant filed sweeping counterclaims, alleging harm caused by the lawsuit.

To try and resolve the matter, I flew in for a settlement conference hosted by the defendant's counsel at his law office. The attorney had put together a slick presentation, complete with a historical over-view of the business, the family members who were running it, and the damage claimed from the case. What was missing? Any attempt to articulate a defense to our claims. Not a single mention—let alone counter—to our evidence was offered.

As counsel worked his way through the presentation, you could tell from his voice and pacing he was building toward a big fin-ish, and that he did. The very last slide regis-tered a number, right out of *Austin Powers* and in poster-board font: $100,000,000.00— the amount they were claiming from us in damages.

Without saying a word, I put my legal pad in my briefcase, excused myself from the room, and departed the office, hailing a cab to the airport to fly back home. There were no further settlement conferences. After the expenditure by the defendant of fair sums of money in legal fees, and prior to trial, the defendant—still absent a defense—agreed to settle; a settlement that included payment of damages for their past counterfeit sales and dismissal of all counterclaims.

- **Don't exhibit, or act out of, desperation.** It is a fact of business and life that the other side does not and will not reward weakness. For example, if you are negotiating or seeking alignment, don't threaten to escalate unless you have the intent and will to do so. On too many occasions, I have witnessed individuals threaten litigation unless their asks were met and then promptly fail to follow through. Similarly, I've been on the receiving end of requests for marketing investments or compensation in various settings by lawyers and businesspeople alike. Without making their case, I've had people say, "You have to give us something" or "I can't go back to my management with that." In fact, I don't and you can. The other person doesn't care about potential repercussions to you or your company, especially if you fail to make the proposal worth their while.

  As you likely have experienced yourself, acting out of desperation or a weak hand guarantees one thing: You will not get what you are looking for and will likely invite more than you bargained for in return. It is your job to take the time to strengthen your hand—mostly through a more informed and diligent study of the issues and your opponent—or to recalibrate your demands and expectations accordingly.

Don't confuse professionalism, transparency, or compromise with weakness. You can be professional, transparent, and conciliatory, while advancing a hard bargain. Weakness, in a negotiation, reflects a failure to prepare or to inform yourself about the needs or motivations of the other side. It embodies overreach and lazy asks and expectations. Very few people will do a deal "at any cost." As seen by the Marriott and Microsoft piracy stories above, sometimes the best thing to do—perhaps due to a breakdown of reason on the other side—is not to do a deal or settle a dispute, but rather to fight. Moreover, failing to maintain a professional demeanor or otherwise taking others' comments, acts, or omissions *personally* will invite distance and conflict that may prove too vast to counter.

These lessons are important for both sides of a negotiation. They reinforce for each of us not to undermine our credibility by shrouding ourselves in the victim cloak, overplaying our hand, or acting out of weakness or desperation, as any one of these behaviors can lead us down the path to failure. They also emphasize that we do not need to accept, nor should we reward, such behaviors when exhibited by the other side.

Noted communications expert Julian Treasure identified what he calls the seven deadly sins of speaking. He lists them as: *Gossip, Judging, Negativity, Complaining, Excuses, Exaggerating/Lying, and Dogmatism.*[22] We will cover this topic in more detail at Chapter 5 Be Accountable and Vulnerable, but I list them here to make the stark distinction between actions and behaviors that are draped in negativity and pessimism versus those that are hopeful and constructive. Yes, we have worked with, and opposite, such folks, some of whom manage to hit all seven in a single sitting. While you don't have the power to change them, you do have the tools to mini-mize, if not neutralize altogether, the decay they can bring to a consensus-building pursuit like a negotiation. The first step is to build your connection with them by appealing to

---

[22] See www.youtube.com/watch?v=eIho2S0ZahI.

and cultivating the positives they bring to the table. Here are some key tips:

Personalize your message

As the title of this chapter states, while you should not take things personally, you should look to personalize your message, as we will get into in much greater detail in Chapter 4, *Show, Don't Tell. Ingrain Your Message.* Recall my encounter with the justice of the Rhode Island Supreme Court or Don Draper's re-brand of the "Carousel." Delivering a personalized message—meaning an appeal to self-interest or human emotion—is a key ingredient for a strengthened human connection and, in turn, winning advocacy.

Connect yourself and your message to their emotional state. Lou Gehrig, the New York Yankee struck down during his Hall of Fame career by a devastating neurological disorder that now bears his name, gave one of the most compelling and memorable speeches of all time. It was under ninety seconds in duration and about three short paragraphs in length. Yet it was brilliantly composed, both in the way he made it personal to himself and relatable to others. It read in part:

"Fans, for the past two weeks you have been reading about the bad break I got. Yet today I consider myself the luckiest man on the face of this earth. . . .

"When the New York Giants, a team you would give your right arm to beat, and vice versa, sends you a gift—that's something. . . . When you have a father and a mother who work all their lives so you can have an education and build your body— it's a blessing. When you have a wife who has been a tower of strength and shown more courage than you dreamed existed—that's the finest I know.

"So I close in saying that I might have been given a bad break, but I've got an awful lot to live for."[23]

Several years back, I was having dinner with the CEO of a medium-sized Chinese PC maker. This was a growing company and there were many opportunities for partnership between our businesses. At one point, we moved into a part-business, part-philosophical discussion about international differences on IP and incentives for innovation. After a few glasses of wine, the CEO turned and said, "It should be remembered that the Chinese invented the compass 2,000 years ago. In turn, every other nation took it from us and

---

[23] See www.lougehrig.com/about/farewell.html.

built it for themselves. Yet we never complained." While not the answer I was hoping for or even all that convincing on the merits, in a few short sentences, he had successfully personalized the conversation and forced me to rethink my approach to introducing joint opportunities.

In one of the most watched TED talks ever, civil rights lawyer and advocate Bryan Stevenson told the story of how he came to discover his special purpose in life. He started by sharing a private moment he had with his grandmother when he was just a child. He recounted that his grandmother explained how greatness awaited him, but that he had to live by three uncompromising rules: (1) always love his mom (her daughter); (2) always do the right thing even when it's the hard thing; and (3) never drink alcohol.

Years later, his older brother was teasing him for continuing to say no to alcohol, letting him in on a family secret that their grandmother had given the exact speech to all of her grandkids. Brushing off the taunt and building toward his main message, Stevenson said:

"I'm 52 years old and I've never had a drop of alcohol. . . . There is power in identity."[24]

As we will cover in much greater detail in Chapter 4, building visual imagery through show-don't-tell illustration is one of your most powerful weapons for personalizing your message and, in turn, for persuasive and winning advocacy.

Demonstrate sincere and active listening. Another critical dimension in *personalizing* your approach is establishing an authentic connection with your counterpart. As discussed throughout this book, the relationship you strike with your audience matters. Particularly when one can choose to do something or not, people will be more committed and will work harder when dealing with someone for whom they feel a genuine attachment.

One of the best ways to connect with others is to demonstrate that you are listening to what they have to say and are giving due weight and consideration to their requests and proposals. Some negotiating experts take the view that you should *never* repeat or acknowledge the opposing side's position,

---

[24] See www.youtube.com/watch?v=c2tOp7OxyQ8.

that doing so needlessly elevates its import. **I disagree.**

I often begin negotiating sessions repeating what I heard from the other side to be their key goals and objectives, as well as their specific proposals around areas of dispute or contention. I don't believe this leads to an anchoring or validation of their position. After all, we still retain our free will even in stressful negotiations. To the contrary, it contributes to a personal connection by showing them you are listening and care about what they have to say, which, importantly, fuels the emotional intangibles for persuading others in a negotiation. It shows empathy.

Summarizing their position also allows me to maintain leadership and control over the negotiation by putting those factors back into my framework for discussing and ultimately aligning on deal terms. It gives me license to construct the type of conditional concessions that we discussed earlier, which demonstrates a willingness to compromise. It also gives me the floor to say "no" to those requests that are either unacceptable or non-negotiable from our perspective, along with the reasons why, at an earlier stage of the negotiation. I have found that a firm and early "no" accompanied by a thoughtful explanation is often better received, if not appreciated, by the other side than a soft "maybe" that later shifts to a "no." This is especially the case when it's perceived by the other side that you were merely kicking the can down the road, never intending sincere consideration of their request.

The behaviors discussed in this chapter serve to positively heighten transparency and the dynamics for productive give-and-take conversations between the parties. Staying positive and free from the baggage of personal offense, with your credibility fully intact, will help limit discord, prevent roadblocks, and guard against misaligned expectations. It also will enable you to maintain leadership and control, continuously returning the discussion back into your structure for a deal.

As I said in Chapter 1, establishing control and leadership does not mean you talk, they listen. It means you take on the accountability to learn—by asking—about their needs and wants. It further requires that you demonstrate an authentic interest in their positions, which can best be accomplished by acknowledging them. Of course, maintaining control of the negotiation likewise requires that you remain in control of your emotions and behaviors. Failure to do so risks surrendering your leadership in guiding the discussion toward the agreement you seek.

Express Tips Chapter 2: Personalize, But Don't Take Personally

- ✓ Move past heated exchanges, *quickly*. No hangover effect.

- ✓ Set expectations. Establish norms of conduct, *upfront*.

- ✓ Identify guiding principles and "must haves" for each side.

- ✓ Keep things professional. Stay focused on ideas, not people.

- ✓ Avoid credibility killers.

  - Don't overreach or overplay your hand.

  - Don't exhibit, or act out of, desperation.

- ✓ Personalize your message.

  - Use show-don't-tell imagery (see Chapter 4).

  - Connect yourself and your message to their emotional state.

  - Demonstrate sincere and active listening.

CONFESSIONS OF A GLOBAL NEGOTIATOR

CHAPTER 3:
Make it (Nearly) Impossible for Them
to Disagree with You.

Make It (Nearly) Impossible for Them to Disagree with You

"Conflict cannot survive without your participation."

—Wayne Dyer

Microsoft President Brad Smith once had a debate with Professor Lawrence Lessig, formerly of Stanford Law School and now of Harvard Law School. The topic was Open Source Software (OSS), a subject about which Lessig had written and lectured extensively and for which he was an outspoken proponent. Smith was there to share a less hardened viewpoint, one that suggested commercial software and OSS could peacefully coexist, if not complement one another.

Smith offered opening remarks, through which he painted a picture of a technology landscape where developers would be broadly supported, if not encouraged, to contribute to the OSS community work product. And increasingly, a key participant in this community would be for-profit companies, such as Microsoft, that charged for their products and services as part of a sustainable business model that incented R&D investment and future innovation. To Smith, it was not an all-or-nothing, winner-take-all proposition. Both models would continue to prosper and, over time, would experience less separation and more integration.[25]

When Smith concluded, Lessig took to the microphone and said something along the lines of:

> *I have to say, since Brad entered this debate, it has become quite boring. Because I have a hard time disagreeing with a single thing he says.*[26]

---

[25] As an aside, the debate was about 15 years ago, and Smith's remarks proved clear-sighted considering Microsoft and other top tech companies' maturing embrace of OSS since then.

[26] I could not locate existing video or a transcript of the debate. The paraphrased quote is based on my best recollection having watched video of the event at the time it was held.

This doesn't, and didn't, mean that Smith's remarks were neutral. Smith advocated a position and vision that reflected the perspective of one of the largest and most successful tech companies in the world. He had a point of view and delivered it. The effectiveness of his remarks was in the construction of his speech, by first identifying common areas of interest for the broadest set of industry participants possible, and then painting a clear and unobjectionable—if not widely desired—portrait of success for the future.

So often we get tripped up on *what* we are saying because of *how* we are saying it. Like the managing director of the ad agency declaring Chinese consumers are motivated by price, if you present *arguable* comments at the outset and draw fire, you won't get to the "what" of your presentation. Avoiding that trap is largely within your control.

Tips for limiting disagreement:

Pose a problem statement to ground others in common areas of interest and action

In June of 1963, President Kennedy delivered a speech in what was then known as West Berlin, steps away from the Berlin Wall, imploring the citizens of that city and the rest of the free world to continue the fight against communism and for freedom for all, everywhere. He drew a visual of the problem, followed by an emotional appeal as to why we all must care about solving it. He said:

"There are many people in the world who really don't understand . . . what is the great issue between the free world and the Communist world.

"Let them come to Berlin.

"There are some who say that communism is the wave of the future.

"Let them come to Berlin . . . .

"While the wall is the most obvious and vivid demonstration of the failures of the Communist system——for all the world to see——we take no satisfaction in it; for it is, as your Mayor has said, an offense not only against history but an offense against humanity, separating families, dividing husbands and wives and brothers and sisters, and dividing a people who wish to be joined together.

"Freedom is indivisible, and when one man is enslaved, all are not free. When all are free, then we can look

*forward to that day when this city will be joined as one
and this country and this great Continent of Europe in
a peaceful and hopeful globe . . . .*

*"All—all free men, wherever they may live, are citizens
of Berlin. And, therefore, as a free man, I take pride in
the words—*

"Ich bin ein Berliner."[27]

Moving words, indeed. Luckily for us we tend to deal in less lofty matters. But the approach by compelling advocates—on all subjects large and small—is nonetheless the same. To command the audience, you must start by answering their question, *why should I care?* It's where it all begins, or, in the case of my "or what" moment, could possibly end.

Be factual. Be fair. No hyperbole

In almost all professions, there are job performance reviews between managers and employees. This is a great test for a manager. As with everything else, there are good approaches and not so good ones. I'll tackle the poor examples of manager feedback. They

---

[27] See www.americanrhetoric.com/speeches/jfkberliner.html.

speak in generalities: "You're not strategic." They exaggerate: "You never hit your numbers" or "You're always late with your reports." They lack proportionality or perspective: "You missed this meeting" without acknowledging time pressures of a major assignment that may have led to it. This will sound familiar to many of us, on the receiving—and perhaps even the delivery—end.

Open-ended, unspecific, and overstated comments invite disagreement, no matter the circumstance or venue. It's sloppy, but fortunately, it's also almost entirely avoidable. How? By keeping things tightly and objectively structured around facts. The more we veer into observation or opinion, the more surface area we create for others to do the same. I've seen this frequently, for example, when a meeting starts with a report out of "guiding principles" to anchor a proposal. The presenter opting for general or subjective principles inevitably draws criticism and dissent. Those who connect principles to concrete and established business priorities—objective in nature—generally are met with nods of approval and a free pass to continue.

To be credible, you must also be perceived as fair. This doesn't mean you should be wishy-washy or lacking in a point of view or self-interest, for you or your company. It suggests you approach others willing and able to acknowledge the merits of their positions, while acknowledging the flaws of your own. You may point out that being fair could mean different things to different people, and you would be correct. In the context of a negotiation, I am equating it to being "principled." In other words, your position is based on objective standards, third party validations, and an expectation for reciprocity and symmetry in deal language. For example, in an employment contract you might see that the employer has defined your status as an "employee at will," meaning you can be terminated at any time for virtually any reason at all. By contrast, you see that they have included a penalty clause (in the form of forfeited compensation) in the event you resign within two years of your start date. In that case, the "deal" lacks reciprocity or symmetry of terms and you would be right to call them on it as unfair or unprincipled.

When I interview someone for a job, I always ask them to provide me with examples of them failing in a prior role. I'm less interested in learning about the specifics than I am their willingness to internalize and own their failures. Similarly, when I serve as a judge in moot court competitions, I ask the students what is the weakest (a) fact and (b) legal argument in their case. If you lack the sincerity and confidence to own up to your shortcomings—and they exist for us all—you will rapidly attract dissension and be well on your way to losing the trust and respect of your audience.

Be constructive. Break the impasse

I'm a bit of a political junky. What interests me most is how pundits and politicians handle emotionally charged topics. A typical cable news program will pit two people, from opposite ends of the spectrum, against each other on a given issue. A kind of *Hunger Games* between talking heads. When I watch them, I immediately start assessing whom I believe to be the more persuasive speaker. The filters I use are the same as those described in this and the prior chapter: How factual are they? How fair or introspective? And do they overreach or exaggerate?

Among the key filters I use to assess a commentator's message and delivery: Are they constructive? For me, the worst advocates are those who unapologetically pound out their talking points. Hardly, if ever, do they acknowledge points well made by the other side, nor do they consider or accept that reasonable people might disagree with their viewpoint. Even more so, they resist movement toward common ground or providing a vision for dislodging the impasse represented by competing opinions. They are a babbling battering ram content to bang heads until the other side gives in or up.

The best advocates are not always right. Importantly, it is not even their objective to always be right. It is to persuade others. Likewise, the best dealmakers are only nominally if at all concerned about winning the debate or proving their points. They measure their success by whether they *get good deals done*. That requires that they not allow themselves or the discussion to get stuck, or that they have a plan to unstick it if it does.

Think of the example of my colleague successfully deploying a reset plan with the business exec. Whether an internal or external audience, there are times when you have to be the bigger person, call a time-out, or even confront personal or organizational dysfunction to advance your talks. A form of the below regroup is the type of conversation you should expect of yourself and those working for you when met, for example, by a personality-led stalemate:

> *Seems we have gotten off on the wrong foot. We've had a few animated meetings now, which unfortunately has blocked progress on what I hope we both can agree is a mutually beneficial opportunity. I want you to know I'm committed to working through these issues and toward*

the best possible outcome. And that I take account-ability to not only maintain a constructive relationship with you, but a productive approach toward successfully advancing our collective work and objectives.

Is that something we both can agree on and commit to?

As an advocate—in politics, business, or other of life's work—it is your job to overcome setbacks and discord. And you deserve little credit until you get there or empty the tank trying.

Be inclusive. Narrow minds and narrow skills are, not surprisingly, self-limiting. By contrast, a broad and inclusive field of vision opens you to a world of possibilities. This is also true in how we communicate.

Do you recall the last time you were in a meeting or at a conference and the presenter spoke about a topic you didn't care about or to an audience you were not a part of? You likely tuned them out. Like the busy CFO, who saw no need for a fancy preamble of the presenter's key message, you also may have resented them for wasting your time.

Do a web search for the most "persuasive" words in the English language. At the top of virtually every list you will find the word "you." This is a healthy reminder for when it is your turn to speak or present. There is *nothing* to be gained by narrowly tailoring your message in a way that disinvites others to care or listen. Consider JFK's powerful message. He didn't speak solely to Germans, to Europeans, or to Americans; he spoke to the entire free world: *"All free men, wherever they may live, are citizens of Berlin."*

Martin Luther King, Jr., in delivering what many believe to be the greatest speech of all time, similarly cast as broad a net as possible. Reflect for a moment on the inclusiveness of his statement:

> *"And when this happens, and when we allow freedom ring, when we let it ring from every village and every hamlet, from every state and every city, we will be able to speed up that day when all of God's children, black men and white men, Jews and Gentiles, Protestants and Catholics, will be able to join hands and sing in the words of the old Negro spiritual:*

> *"Free at last! Free at last!*

> *"Thank God Almighty, we are free at last!"*[28]

---

[28] See www.americanrhetoric.com/speeches/mlkihavea dream.htm.

The first and most important step in influencing others is to include them. It also just might be the easiest.

International nuance and sensibilities matter

I lived and worked in Europe for four years. I recall my first trip to Waitrose supermarket in the UK. It looked mostly familiar. Fruits and vegetables at one end; bread, dairy, and meat at the other; and gray processed foods in between. I soon learned it was different. Within minutes of each other I made the missteps of asking a stocking clerk where I could find the English muffins (they're called white muffins) and requesting sliced American cheese (there was no such thing) from the deli counter.

When working internationally and with international companies, you need to accept that you are going to make mistakes and likely will never master local customs or culture no matter how much time you spend there. That does not mean you should ignore or underestimate them. The ad agency lead who flopped his pitch to the Microsoft China team couldn't change the fact that he was American. But he could have presented his core thesis (that Chinese consumers are motivated by price) differently to minimize objection. He could have spent more time describing his methodology and the due diligence by his firm—and Chinese co-workers—in validating their research-backed assumptions. Speaking as a non-local in China to a Chinese audience in English, invoking what seemed to be poorly researched assumptions about local buying behavior, was a recipe for disaster and ultimately too much for him to overcome.

Perhaps the most important thing you can do to try and bridge a cultural divide is to demonstrate a sincere interest in learning about the people, the history, and the unique characteristics of the country or region. Above all, ask questions. Be curious. When I was living in Europe, I managed legal affairs for more than fifteen company subsidiaries and travelled extensively. My most informative experiences were the cab rides between airports, hotels, and our offices. Cabbies abroad were all too willing to answer my questions and engage in dialogue on everything from the economy, political campaigns, or scandals, and—perhaps the most fascinating—hostilities between neighboring nations, which in Europe typically involved past periods of war and occupation. It's also true what they say: It is genuinely appreciated when you even try a few words in their local tongue.

I'm not sure any foreigner is equipped to provide an exhaustive guide to doing business overseas, and I'm no exception. What I can do, however, is share a quick list of things I learned—often the hard way—from my experiences; things that had I known of and internalized more quickly would have allowed me to pare down the potential areas for disagreement with my audiences:

- **One size doesn't fit all.** While Americans tend to welcome public recognition for a job well done, that isn't necessarily the case for other nationalities where attention given in such a setting could be uncomfortable or even embarrassing. Ask your employees and test the waters before you give them a victory lap. I learned this from a British colleague, who somewhat reluctantly confided about his preference for a more low-key method for my recognizing his good work.

- **As you might expect, some cultures are more relationship-oriented than others.** This is not a good vs. bad observation, but to note that e-mail connections with a colleague in Finland may be sufficient for establishing a good working relationship, whereas a flight to Lisbon and a conversation over lunch may be required to build a connection with a Portuguese colleague.

- **Reciprocate compliments.** On a few occasions, I glossed over comments from co-workers in China that they had received feedback from my peer on the other side of a deal that he or she *respected* me. As I came to learn, this wasn't just a polite or passing comment to be overlooked. It signified they trusted me and felt comfortable working with me. I also learned that it was equally important for me to return the compliment. Expressions of gratitude and respect can mean more than you realize in the right context and with the right audience. Acknowledge and pay back the compliment.

- **Communication styles vary greatly across, and even within, continents.** Some people are indirect, often to maintain politeness, burying their meaning or message deep in an e-mail or after a long introduction in a face-to-face discussion. Others, like the Dutch, just go for it. A Dutch colleague joked with me once that every Dutch baby receives truth serum at birth, which is why they are so forthcoming and linear in their speech. As an East Coaster, I felt right at home.

- **Saving face in Asia is real and it matters.** In Asia, boxing someone in, leaving them little room to maneuver or recover, can be counterproductive. For Americans saving face is more about protecting ego; for Asians it takes on deeper meaning, implicating virtues like dignity and honor. Winning the argument at that stage must take a back seat in favor of inviting their input on a third way of solving the issue.

- **Respect formalities.** Don't downplay or underestimate the importance of preserving and respecting formalities of a given culture. I was a participant in numerous press events in China and learned quickly that they tend to come with various elegant trimmings, things usually dispensed with in the US. Formal introductions, complete with powerful and sophisticated music in the background (think *Chariots of Fire*), with hand-selected floral arrangements adorning the stage and corsages pinned on the lapels of the principals. These are special events and should be appreciated as such. Similarly, know that the exchange of cards or the sequence of opening remarks in Japan (the host always kicks off the meeting), or the invitation to use first names by leaders at customary German companies, come from a place of deep tradition, the intent of which is to create a climate of mutual trust and respect. Embrace such formalities.

- **Be careful using colloquialisms abroad.** I was at a legal proceeding in Brussels. One of the litigants had just completed an eloquent summary of their case. Opposing counsel— who had spent many years living and working in the US—stood, chuckled a bit, and started out by saying, *"My mother always told me you can put lipstick on a pig. But it's still a pig."* The stunned—even horrified—look on the faces in the courtroom was nearly unanimous.

- **Be patient.** I was discussing a business proposal with another company in China a few years ago. It involved a new fiscal year program we were implementing, and it soon became clear we were more interested in pursuing it than they were. My counterpart told me that they would not chase this opportunity, as they needed more time to think it through, adding, *"In the US, you think about things in terms of quarters or fiscal years. In China, we think about things in terms of decades or centuries."* Always be careful of pushing an initiative faster than your audience can cope with it. Sometimes, you just need to *slow down*.

Building on the first two chapters, this chapter is intended to highlight a common core found across the most persuasive communicators and the best presenters, salespeople, and negotiators. Each is masterful at both limiting the surface area for dissent by their audience and delivering the most widely appealing message possible. They inhibit distractions from their message by maintaining credibility and not suffering from insecurity or personal offense. And they reflect on international dynamics and implications when engaging foreign audiences.

Use this test to ensure you've made it difficult for others to disagree with you

Before sending an important e-mail or polishing content for a key presentation, inspect it, searching for distracting subjectivity and gray areas that will invite conflict. If you find it, eliminate it. Watch for adjectives, superlatives, or hyperbole. Also, rid your work of unnecessary emotional outbursts or personal shots that stagnate the conversation around a problem, rather than work to solve it. Think of the most objective, fairest-minded, and principled person you know, and ask yourself, would they have reason to object to anything you've said? If the answer is yes, get back to work. Persuasion only happens when you have accessed the attention, interest, and beliefs of others. Avoid complicating what already stands out as a formidable task by eliminating that with which one can easily disagree.

Express Tips Chapter 3: Make It (Nearly) Impossible for Them to Disagree with You

✓ Pose a problem statement to ground others in common areas of interest and action.

✓ Be factual. Be fair. No hyperbole.

✓ Be constructive. Break the impasse.

✓ Be inclusive.

✓ International nuance and sensibilities matter. Consider:

- One size doesn't fit all.

- Some cultures are more relationship-oriented than others.

- Reciprocate compliments. Expressions of gratitude and respect can mean more than you realize in the right context and with the right audience.

- Communication styles vary greatly across continents and even within continents.

- Saving face in Asia is real and it matters.

- Respect formalities.

- Be careful using colloquialisms abroad.

- Be patient. Sometimes you just need to slow down.

✓ Use a simple test to ensure you've made it difficult for them to disagree with you.

CONFESSIONS OF A GLOBAL NEGOTIATOR

CHAPTER 1:
It Starts with You. *You* set the tone.

CHAPTER 2:
Personalize, But Don't Take Personally.

CHAPTER 3:
Make it (Nearly) Impossible for Them
to Disagree with You.

CHAPTER 4:
Show, Don't Tell. Ingrain Your Message.

Show, Don't Tell. Ingrain Your Message

"There's always room for a story that can transport people to another place."

—J. K. Rowling

I had an executive review once on a project I had initiated in Southern China to build a closer connection to an emerging market of device makers that seemed to have developed overnight. I had thirty minutes and lots to pull from that I could cover. In fact, too much. I could have used all my time providing a historical overview of the locale. Shenzhen was a small farming town twenty short years ago. Since that time, it has developed into a metropolis of manufacturing, organized by district. It has a leather district, a semiconductor district, a TV district, an automotive district, and many others. For miles into the distance, all you see are high-rise apartments next to sprawling factories and campuses. A sure-thing destination for the young from underserved Tier 4 and 5 cities to come land jobs, the city now boasts an estimated population of more than 12 million, up from maybe 30,000 just a few decades ago.

I also had content to cover on the companies that were emerging there, from carmakers to silicon providers, from phone OEMs to home-automation suppliers. We had data and forecasts and revenue projections. After pulling together a briefing deck, heavy on analytics, I decided on a different path. I opted to simplify the discussion. This was a unique market. Racing to the business plan, I feared, would obscure what truly made it so.

I prepared three slides, made up mostly of photos I had taken on my last trip. The title slide contained nothing more than a picture of the sign that welcomes you to Shenzhen International Airport. Out of all the information I could have drawn from to set the context, the quote on the sign did the best job of capturing the essence of the city. It read:

"Time is Money, Efficiency is Life."

The story behind this quote was told through the pictures I then shared of the marketplace of componentry that ran throughout the city, where manufacturers of nearly anything and everything would come to source their parts, haggling on price down to the smallest denomination. It was an atmosphere not unlike that experienced at a Saturday-morning Turkish bazaar, except the finished products from this marketplace ended up as 360-degree cameras, drones, and 4K OLED TVs stocked for sale at Apple stores, Costco, and Walmart.

With these visual images established, the rest of the discussion was a breeze.

The art of storytelling can be learned

I am a linear thinker and writer. When I worked at a law firm, my earliest writing, I'm sure, reflected this and perhaps it still does. I am the person I described earlier from the Project Insights assessment: *Be Brief, Be Bright, Be Gone.* It has become a learned behavior for me to think in terms of storytelling and visualization over brute "logic." While the numbers stacked up making a Shenzhen initiative well worth pursuing—and I was tempted to hammer away at them—this was an example of the importance of embracing life-long growth, both as a person and as a communicator.

Chapter 1 explains that being an effective and persuasive communicator takes work. It takes thought. And it takes preparation. It doesn't come naturally to most of us. You must be willing to commit yourself to trying new things, learning from others, and taking risks.

I once worked with a marketing leader, who was among the top presenters I'd ever seen. He was entertaining, commanding, and a great storyteller. He was someone you were sure could get out of bed each day ready to pitch anything to anyone.

At an external event once, I saw that he and I were back-to-back speakers, with him preceding me. Awesome, I thought, this surely was going to crater my speaker feedback scores. Before it was his time to present, I left the convention room to get some water. Outside in the hallway, I spotted my colleague, pacing back and forth, speaking to himself. As I got closer, I realized he wasn't speaking to himself at all, but rather was rehearsing his talk. He was so focused he didn't even see me. He had his printed speech in hand that he would occasionally glance down at. In working with him for several years, I had never once seen him consult a script or even notes in meetings, technical demos, or presentations. I became flush with insecurities. If *he* needed a script and a rehearsal, I was doomed.

About a week after the event, I ran into him at the office and asked him about his extra preparation for his talk, as I always regarded him a natural. He shared that he had severe anxieties around public speaking earlier in his career, and to a certain extent, still did. The antidote, he said, was preparation. Only when he felt he was truly prepared—meaning constructing great slides, developing a theme, weaving in stories to entertain and paint a picture for the audience, and rehearsing, a lot—could he feel comfortable. And he repeated this process every time he spoke or presented in public, before large and small audiences alike.

Memorable messaging taps into the truths of human nature

Storytelling and building visual images are severely overlooked and underutilized. Yet, they are an absolutely essential ingredient to effective and persuasive communication. And by storytelling, I am referring, in the broader sense, to a show-don't-tell approach to descriptive expression. Young writers often struggle with mastering the dreaded show-don't-tell style, encouraged by their teachers to employ sensory language that goes beyond the facts and conveys feeling. But embracing this nuanced communications skill serves the patient student throughout their life. Consider that people are spoken to and at all day long. The competition for registering an idea or comment with their busy brains is fierce. Storytelling, rather than just telling, is compelling and memorable. Storytelling, as someone once said, is "data with a soul."[29]

Chris Herren was a star basketball player from Durfee High School in Fall River, Massachusetts, and later played for the Boston Celtics in the 1990s. ESPN did a segment on him called "Unguarded" as part of its "30 for 30" documentary series.[30] It wasn't solely, or even mostly, about his basketball talents. It was about his decade-long nightmare of drug addiction that almost cost him everything.

The segment, which I believe to be the very best of all the ESPN documentaries (and there have been some exceptional ones) and perhaps the most compelling take I've ever seen on addiction, was a true illustration of the power of show-don't-tell

---

[29] Brene Brown. See www.youtube.com/watch?v=iCvms MzlF7o

[30] See *Unguarded* vimeo.com/79305689.

storytelling, with Herren as storyteller-in-chief. A husband and father to a loving wife and children, Herren now tours the country speaking to audiences that include high school students, inmates, college and professional athletes, and law enforcement and military personnel, explaining the annihilating effects of his abusive behavior on himself, but more significantly, on his family and anyone who ever cared for him.

A few excerpts from his story:

"I've had four overdoses and seven felonies for drugs . . . . I woke up [once from an overdose] with an ambulance driver telling me 'you've been dead for 30 seconds' . . .

"I spent every dime I ever made in basketball on drugs. I spent every dime my wife ever made [on drugs]. I robbed every toy my kids ever had . . . . Here I am a big-time basketball player—been in Rolling Stone, Sports Illustrated, the NBA, Boston Celtics, Denver Nuggets, and overseas, and I'm on a street corner hocking [my wife's] jewelry while [she] was raising two kids and eight-months pregnant."[31]

---

[31] Id.

By the end of his talk, there is no need for him to say, "Don't do drugs" or "Just say no." You had experienced the journey through his living nightmare right there with him. Nothing more needed to be said, just like with civil rights lawyer Bryan Stevenson. Stevenson, I'm sure, could have talked at length about how much he adored his grandmother and how he would have done anything for her. Instead, through his honest and human storytelling, he showed us.

Find the compelling story in your argument

While personal, emotion-inducing stories capture the audience's attention, storytelling and building a visual image for others works in almost any context. I was once analyzing a senior exec's proposal for a Windows pricing program in developing markets. Part of my job was to ensure we had proper controls in place in administering the program to avoid unintended consequences, including leakage of the discounted price into developed markets. This involved me testing the program against various scenarios where problems might arise, ranging in likelihood from possible to remote. Understandably, as a person with considerable P&L responsibilities, he was feeling a sense of urgency. And I could sense him becoming impatient with what appeared to him as my overly cautious approach.

As I prepared for a meeting with him to report on some interim findings, I was thinking how best to explain that while it may appear I was too slow or conservative in my approach, the steps were necessary to get us to the final stages. But I also wanted him to know I was firmly committed to supporting his initiative. As they say, talk is cheap, so I tried a different approach. I knew he was a hockey fan, so I included the following quote from Wayne Gretzky on the title slide of the presentation:

"100% of the shots you don't take don't go in."

By my acknowledgement and embrace of his bias for action, he received this as the olive branch I intended it to be. Through tighter alignment and a strengthened relationship, we moved on and finalized the project.

So why don't people use this technique more frequently? I'm not sure. Perhaps it takes them outside their zone of comfort, or they believe it is too risky or not serious enough. What I have seen in its place is a predictable fallback on a string of adjectives as the mechanism of choice for conveying emotion. I recall walking down the hallway of my law firm as a new associate. In a corner office sat one of the senior partners, and I overheard him dictating a letter into his handheld recorder (yes, I am dating myself, but then again, we were lawyers, notorious laggards on technology). In a booming voice, he started, "I am amazed and shocked . . ." He stopped the recording, rewound it, and started over again, "I am shocked and amazed." Pleased with the change, he continued.

Chris Herren would attract audiences even if he used the time to say that his addiction caused him to be a "terrible dad and husband." But it's his storytelling of having sold his kids' PlayStation and every other possession in the house with even a trace of value—down to the vacuum cleaner—that captures you and pulls you in to his life story. Storytelling in its broadest sense is an expansive tool that favors illustration over just telling. It is a bit like virtual reality (which takes you to a whole new world) and augmented reality (which keeps you in your world but extends it with enhanced imagery) combined.

Storytelling can involve a parable, a historical example, or something that happened to you. It also can be the quote from Shenzhen or Wayne Gretzky. It can even be a question out of left field that forces deep introspection. It's whatever allows the listener or reader to generate a mental picture of the idea or meaning you are trying to convey. It ingrains the message in their brains. And that is often the extra nudge needed to influence people.

I will take my own advice, and do more showing and less telling. Below are examples of a few of my favorite visual images, illustrations, quotes, and questions. I'm sure you have your own.

Performance improvement advice: *"Do you like what you do?"*

This was a question I was asked by a PR lead after I did a press conference years ago. I answered, "Yes, why?" to which she replied, "You don't seem like you're having much fun up there." Translation: Show enthusiasm, smile at least occasionally, and maintain your energy level. Her gentle feedback landed a direct hit to my ego, but her message has stuck with me *every time* I speak to an audience.

Advice from a salesperson: *"Smile right before you take or make a call."*

This was a technique shared by a salesperson. He said that when he starts off a conversation with a smile, he ensures his sales calls begin on a happy and upbeat note. He could have *told* us to always have enthusiasm and joy for your work. He *showed* us how he does it instead.

More advice from a salesperson: *"On a scale of 1-10, how competitive are you?"*

This was a question a sales leader and colleague asked every time he interviewed someone for a role in his group. He added that, "If they don't say 9 or 10, I don't hire them." My colleague was looking for a show-don't-tell answer so he asked a show-don't-tell question.

Advice on taking pride in work: *"Whatever you are, be a good one."*

A famous quote by Abraham Lincoln. I love it for its simplicity and expanse; it applies to everyone and to every dimension of life.

Pure imagery:

- *"The Rangers looked up and saw the enemy soldiers at the edge of the cliffs, shooting down at them with machine guns and throwing grenades. And the*

American Rangers began to climb. They shot rope ladders over the face of these cliffs and began to pull themselves up. When one Ranger fell, another would take his place. When one rope was cut, a Ranger would grab another and begin his climb again. They climbed, shot back, and held their footing. Soon, one by one, the Rangers pulled themselves over the top, and in seizing the firm land at the top of these cliffs, they began to seize back the continent of Europe."[32] (Ronald Reagan)

- *"And you know, if I were standing at the beginning of time, with the possibility of taking a kind of general and panoramic view of the whole of human history up to now, and the Almighty said to me, 'Martin Luther King, which age would you like to live in?' I would take my mental flight by Egypt and I would watch God's children in their magnificent trek from the dark dungeons of Egypt . . . across the Red Sea, through the wilderness on toward the promised land. And in spite of its magnificence, I wouldn't stop there."[33]* (Martin Luther King)

---

[32] Ronald Reagan, commemorating the 40th anniversary of D-Day. See www.americanrhetoric.com/speeches/ronaldreaganddayaddress.html.

[33] Martin Luther King, *"I've Been to the Mountaintop" speech*. See www.americanrhetoric.com/speeches/mlkivebeentothemountaintop.htm.

- *"Never do you feel more at one with your bike than when you are descending. When the magic is in the air, there is a beautiful flow to the ride. You are water curving through a hose."[34]* (Geraint Thomas, cyclist)

As done masterfully by Chris Herren, the authors here invite you in as a front-row passenger on a journey, with all that that entails—the majesty, emotions, pain, and discovery of the experience.

Thought provoking:

- *"Death very likely is the single best invention of life. It's life's change agent. It clears out old to make room for new. You will be old one day. Your time is limited. Don't waste it living someone else's life."[35]* (Steve Jobs)

- *"We have achieved most as surgeons when our patients recover completely and forget us completely. All patients are immensely grateful at first after a*

---

[34] See *The World of Cycling According to G* by Geraint Thomas (2015) at page 133.

[35] Steve Jobs' commencement speech at Stanford. See www.youtube.com/watch?v=UF8uR6Z6KLc&t=539s.

successful operation but if the gratitude persists it usually means that they have not been cured . . . and they fear they may need us in the future . . . We have been most successful, however, when our patients return to their homes and get on with their lives and never need to see us again. They are grateful, no doubt, but happy to put us and the horror of their illness behind them. Perhaps they never quite realized just how dangerous the operation had been and how lucky they were to have recovered so well. Whereas the surgeon, for a while, has known heaven, having come very close to hell."[36] (Henry Marsh, Neurosurgeon)

These are penetrating concepts and images that leave the reader vulnerable yet intrigued, wanting for more meaning by turning the words inward for their own self-discovery.

As reflected, there are many ways to illustrate a point of view or message. While it may lack the artistry or weight of, say, metaphoric or historic reference—or the pure imagery of the cycling or D-Day quotes above—the use of a well-timed question is one of my favorite tools for registering an

---

[36] See *Do No Harm: Stories of Life, Death, and Brain Surgery* by Henry Marsh (2016) at page 34.

idea or point. When you are asked, "Do you like what you do?"—with clear purpose intended by the person asking—it stops you in your tracks, freezing you with uncertainty. It forces immediate and uninterrupted introspection, and it is something you remember and take with you. That is the very essence of ingraining your message through show-don't-tell imagery.

A good storyteller can spot weak narratives

I was leading a negotiation once with a very seasoned business leader on the other side. He spent the first ten minutes of a follow-up meeting touching on a new proposal they had received from a competitor of ours. He then spent the next ten minutes attacking the value proposition of our product offering, which formed a key part of the deal we were negotiating. It was a well-prepared argument, but it seemed to come out of nowhere as we had been making steady and positive strides toward a deal. I sat back for a moment, not entirely clear where this all left us. So, I decided to put the onus on him, using a tool much like the PR lead employed with me. I said words to the effect of:

> *I take you at your word on the economic advantages of the offer you're contemplating from our competitor, and I also can see your thoughtful preparation*

in describing the comparative drawbacks in our product offer and functionality. I'm reminded though that you insisted on this further meeting. I guess the only question I have is if the competitive offer was that attractive—one which you know we will not try and match—and our product is so lacking, then, respectfully, why are we here and what is left to discuss?

I had calculated that this was more positioning on his part than a walk-from-the-table event, based on his demonstrated commitment to date for a deal. I also reflected that his behavior in pitching this in what felt to be a clinical and somewhat dispassionate manner, was an iterative, rather than bottom-line moment in the negotiation. I was correct. The question prompted him to reaffirm his reasons for and continued interest in a deal with us. From there we moved on, advancing our search for common ground.

We learn the greatest lessons in life from others. Be a student. Look for and give thought to that which touches your emotions. Whether you are giving a speech in front of hundreds or thousands, or a presentation to a few, think in advance of the most important messages you want to deliver, and then construct your version of the Shenzhen or Wayne Gretzky quote, or the PR or sales leader's questions, and land it.

Express Tips Chapter 4: Show, Don't Tell. Ingrain Your Message

- ✓ Illustrate. Be a storyteller.

- ✓ The art of storytelling can be learned.

- ✓ Memorable messaging taps into the truths of human nature.

- ✓ Find the compelling story in your argument.

- ✓ A good storyteller can spot weak narratives.

- ✓ Construct your best visual and land it.

CONFESSIONS OF A GLOBAL NEGOTIATOR

Chapter 5

Be Accountable
and Vulnerable

*"You are not a failure until you start blaming
others for your mistakes."*
—John Wooden

P eople sometimes will ask of others, what is the best advice you ever received? In my case, it wasn't advice, it was a lesson.

When I was a junior in high school, I played JV basketball. A good friend and teammate came to me one day and asked if I'd be interested in going on a double date to a school dance that Friday night. The only problem was we had a basketball game that evening. Applying the logic and decision-making rigor of your typical seventeen-year-olds, we went to our coach and told him we would have to miss the game to attend the dance. I recall our coach asking what kind of dance it was, knowing it wasn't our class prom, which wouldn't be for a few months still. We said it was a school dance, but one of the important ones—like a required event—and that all juniors would be going. (I'd like to be able to qualify this as a white lie but I can't. It was a flat-out fabrication.)

Our coach nodded his head and said simply, "Well, it seems you have given this some thought and decided to do this, so there's nothing left to say." The dance—which was fine—came and went, and we prepared for our next game, which was mid-week the following week.

As he did before every game, our coach wrote down the starting lineup and talked about match-ups with the other team. My friend and I were starters, but not this time. Nowhere on the board did we see our names. When the game began, we sat. And we sat. Our names were not called in the first or second quarter, or anytime thereafter. We ended the game on the bench in our warm-ups, never once breaking a sweat. After the game, which we lost, the coach, as he always did post-game, discussed the most significant player and team stats. He started this one out a little differently, though. He turned to his assistant coach and asked how many assists my friend and fellow benchwarmer had. He asked how many points he had.

Coach then shifted and asked how many rebounds I contributed and how many offensive charges I took. *None* was the answer received for each-and-every question.

I recall taking the bus home that night feeling a bit angry and a lot embarrassed. It felt then like an overreaction, and the locker room shaming unnecessary. The next game arrived, and the same treatment awaited us. We didn't start. We didn't play. And the assistant coach, again, publicly announced zero after zero next to our names as part of the end-of-game stat review.

Enough time has passed since these events occurred that I honestly don't recall if it was two or three games that we were benched. It doesn't really matter. Many years later, those few games remain the single most vivid and powerful lesson on accountability I've experienced. And I think back on those moments—and privately thank my coach for them—often to this day.

Be accountable

Webster's defines accountability as *"[a]n obligation or willingness to accept responsibility or to account for one's action.*[37] Accountability is the centerpiece for success whether in sports, business, or relationships. Synovus Bank—a small, mostly anonymous company chartered in Columbus, Georgia—routinely places in annual published lists of best companies to work for. According to its CEO and employees, it comes down to their corporate philosophy, summed up in two numbers: 100 / 0. The first number stands for 100% accountability and the second for 0% excuses.[38]

Accountability is similarly required of us in our business interactions and dealings, the absence of which can end relationships or business opportunities, and, even worse, permanently tarnish reputations. It comes down to a simple concept: *Say what you will do and do what you say.* It's about being transparent with the other side and taking ownership when you are wrong, have misled them (intentionally or not), or simply failed to deliver on a commitment.

---

[37] See www.merriam-webster.com/dictionary/accountability.

[38] See www.youtube.com/watch?v=2F0PFauQynQ&index=2 &list=PLNuGS6rPleK82M9DnvfspnOLz60jryCQP.

Tips on *accountability:*

- **Adhere to your *norms of conduct* discussed in Chapter 2.** Defining what the other side can expect from you is the first step toward limiting conflict or dissent. Being accountable by following through on your commitments is required thereafter.

- **Be timely.** Especially in a deal context, establishing and maintaining trust with the other side is essential. One of the best ways of doing so is demonstrating your respect for their time. Stick to set conference calls and meeting times, and be on time. When you take on an action item, try and provide a timeframe for completion or even an update. But when you do that, deliver on it.

- **Be responsive.** I once had a manager who lived by a cardinal rule: Unless there were matters beyond his control, he would respond to e-mails the *same day* in which he received them. Even if his response was just a quick note to let you know he was traveling or dealing with an emergency, holding true to it was a matter of character and integrity for him. Here's what that commitment meant to me as an employee: It signaled that he cared about me and my work every bit as much as he did himself and his work; and that he was investing in my success by helping solve problems at their earliest possible moment and not allowing key decisions to stall.

This experience helped shape my views on the power of responsiveness. It goes well beyond an expression of courtesy. It demonstrates that you care, which is welcome and meaningful whether directed toward an employee, manager, colleague, or an adversary in a negotiation. In fact, it has led me to redefine the standard for what it means to have *trust* or a *trusted relationship* with someone else. Traditionally, I would have defined it as whether I could believe what they were telling me or that they would come through on what they've committed. But it's more than that: Trust also captures the notion that *I will accept and treat as important that which is important to you, with an expectation that you will do the same for me*. A breakdown by either side on this will ultimately lead to a breakdown in trust.

So, for purposes of your engagements with others, try and embrace the same-day rule. Also, be amenable to their proposed *norms of conduct*, such as my peer in a negotiation who asked me to commit to a weekly 1-1 call to ensure we maintained progress and fought through bottlenecks. Above all, recognize that you will be judged by your conduct—not your words—and let your conduct demonstrate that you respect them and are invested in their success.

- **Go above and beyond expectations.** It was once said, "It is not only what we do, but also what we do not do, for which we are accountable."[39] Much of the above is what we can expect of ourselves and others, at a baseline level, in a relationship. But over-delivery is the mark of success, and a hallmark of over-delivery is excelling at open and transparent communication.

  It should be noted that you should never put yourself or your company in a position where you reveal too much information, including any information that is confidential. There are some on the other side

---

[39] Quote from Jean-Baptiste Poquelin, known by his stage name Molière.

of a negotiation I've worked with who love to provide a play-by-play of their latest discussions with their executives, and provide insight into certain developments or initiatives not yet made public. This shouldn't be encouraged or rewarded. It reflects badly on the other person and you shouldn't be complicit. With that understanding, there is a balance that can be met that demonstrates a level of candor and transparency that goes beyond minimum expectations.

For example, rather than provide details about an internal exec sync, you should consider sharing that an exec meeting has or will be taking place at which time your initiative or deal will be discussed. It might also be appropriate to provide some insight into your perspective and contribution as part of that meeting, which you set up to achieve internal consensus around the proposal the parties have been discussing. It reinforces that you and your company are taking the deal seriously. It also shows you are taking an active role in advancing the internal conversation and decision-making in furtherance of the joint work and interests between you and your peer.

- **Own up to your mistakes.** I had a recent situation where we were getting down to a short list of open issues we needed to clear on a deal. There was one such issue that remained on the list at the insistence of the other side. It wasn't a big item, in my mind, nor was it something I felt was a potential deal breaker. In the interest of narrowing our list, I cavalierly suggested that we might be able to resolve that issue largely in line with their recommendation, and we should set it aside for the moment. This, I thought, would allow us to focus on what I viewed as the larger pending items and might create some goodwill toward potential compromises from their end on the more significant issues. Unfortunately, I hadn't properly vetted or investigated the proposed solution for the more *minor* item. Indeed, I learned later that day when I looked into it that we simply couldn't deliver on it.

  I called my peer that night to share the news that I had spoken prematurely and that we could not solve it as proposed after all. While he appreciated the transparency and my prompt follow-up, he was not happy that the issue was added back, especially as I seemed confident it could be resolved. I had a choice at that point. I could have asked him to put this in some context and that I too had been disappointed by his or his team's behaviors at various points in our negotiations, involving matters that exceeded mine in terms of size and significance. Would that have met Synovus's 100 / 0 standard? Or my own heightened definition of *trust*? The answer is *no* and *no*. I recall gathering myself a bit and saying something as follows:

> *You have reason to be disappointed. I was wrong. Not in ultimately deciding that we couldn't agree to your proposed solution; deciding otherwise would compound the issue when we under-delivered down the road. I was wrong in my failure to take this item as seriously as I should have; in my failure to set the right expectations; and in my failure to do the due diligence required before signaling our directional alignment.*

With that, we got back to work.

Be vulnerable

Admitting one's mistakes is an example of being *vulnerable*. As I started to write this section, I couldn't clear from my mind the image I had of "The Fonz"—the tough, cool character from the TV show *Happy Days*—in one episode confronting his near-physical inability to acknowledge his errors. "I was wrrrrr . . ." he would start. After a few tries he'd get to, "I was wrrrooo . . ." Suffice it to say, *wrong* didn't quite roll off his tongue.

We all are born with a defense mechanism by which we try and shield others from easily detecting our flaws. The Socratic method employed in law school was particularly ruthless at penetrating that shield. It involved the law professor picking a name from the class list and peppering that person with questions—from discreet facts in a case to hypotheticals, or "hypos," as they were called—mostly with the goal of achieving victory in the form of the retreating student offering up a mounting series of I-don't-knows. Some professors chose to spread the pain by moving quickly from one student to the next, ensuring no one was comfortably beyond their reach.

In my very first class on my very first day in law school, my torts professor initiated us into this right-of-passage that would stalk us every class thereafter over our three-year education. Without as much as a welcome or an introduction, he kicked off our legal careers by calling out the name of a classmate, which was plain and ordinary sounding, likely to minimize the possibility of messing up the pronunciation. (Most law school professors have first-class egos, and are not very good at being *vulnerable*.) The student stood up. He did not sit again for the remainder of the fifty-minute class.

The professor started with a rather pedestrian fact pattern about assault and battery, reeling my classmate in with a false sense of confidence. Little by little, he changed the facts, to make it less obviously fit within what we, as novices, believed assault and battery to be. He asked:

> *"What if I didn't hit you with a bat, but instead put a radio up to your ear and turned the volume up to ten (yes, imagery of the boom box should come to mind for Gen Xers) and it hurt your eardrum? Is that assault and battery?"*

> *"What if it didn't hurt your eardrum, but it scared and annoyed you?"*

"What if I put the radio down and decided to spit at you?"

"What if I spit at you and nothing came out, but you felt the wind blow past your face?"

One after the other, each hypothetical tougher than the one preceding it, the professor continued, for the entire class. When it was time to move on to our next class, we all stepped aside for our physically and emotionally spent classmate to exit, each of us feeling sorry for him, but more selfishly experiencing a sense of relief our name was just a little harder to pronounce than his that day.

We live in a tough and challenging world and lead complex lives. We are not without flaws and should not expect to be. If others can accept that of us, why can't we?

Before I go much further, you may be thinking:

Hold on, the last piece of advice I'd ever expect on negotiating is to make yourself vulnerable.

But that's exactly what you should do. If there is one central message to this book, it's that *your behavior,* including your emotional conduct, is the single most powerful asset—within your control—for determining success or failure in persuading others. Establishing and maintaining credibility, both as a competent professional and as a trusted source, is an essential part of that. And humanizing yourself, by allowing yourself to be vulnerable, is an essential part of establishing credibility.

Brené Brown is a leading researcher, who has studied vulnerability and how it, as well as the absence of it, affects us personally and professionally. Her studies show that people with feelings of self-worth tend to establish more meaningful and enduring relationships, and an attribute common among these individuals is the ability to embrace vulnerability.[40] She describes vulnerability as *"shame and fear, but also as the birthplace of joy and belonging."*[41] She paints a picture of a world without vulnerability as a place where we:

- make the uncertain certain (think of the "I'm right, you're wrong" certainties in politics today);

- try to be perfect—(ourselves and our children); and

---

[40] See www.youtube.com/watch?v=iCvmsMzlF7o&t=257s.
[41] Id.

- pretend—that what we do has no impact on others.[42]

She continues by illustrating a picture of a society where vulnerability is ever present. Where we:

- let ourselves be seen, deeply seen, vulnerably seen;

- love with our whole hearts; and

- practice gratitude and joy.[43]

One can see the sincerity and authenticity of the person and society embracing vulnerability. It tells the other person: I will admit my mistakes, and say I am sorry when I am wrong; I will work to confront and fix problems, not hide them or from them; and I will express thanks to you for doing the same.

In the Chris Herren documentary, there is a part where he talks about a breakthrough in his sobriety and his feeling of belonging once again with his wife and kids. He said during his darkest days he had developed the habit of shaving and brushing his teeth

---

[42] Id.

[43] Id.

in the shower. One day after he had settled back in with his family, his wife asked why she never finds his razor and toothbrush in the shower anymore. Herren replied:

> *"Because I can finally look at myself in the mirror (again)."*[44]

The interviewee who humblebrags their way through the question, "Can you give me a few examples of your failing in a prior role" with gems like, "I cared too much" or "I had a hard time saying no," neglects to "let themselves be seen, deeply seen." Perceptions of insecurity and inauthenticity set in, while reliability and trust are forced out. Like the lawyer who acknowledges no weak points in their case or an individual who accepts no role in a failed relationship, invulnerability clouds believability, and waning believability breeds mistrust.

It has been said that "vulnerability is not about winning or losing. It's about having the courage to show up and be seen."[45] Never was this more true than with Scott Norwood, a professional kicker for the Buffalo Bills who missed a 47-yard field goal as

---

[44] See www.vimeo.com/79305689.

[45] See www.youtube.com/watch?v=iCvmsMzlF7o&t=257s.

time expired that would have secured a victory over the New York Giants in Super Bowl XXV. Field goal kickers are specialists on a football team, called on to perform a single function: to kick the football through the goal posts, oftentimes in exceptionally pressure-filled situations. After the game, Norwood stood by his locker to meet the press and stayed until every interview was completed. Every possible incarnation of "How do you feel?" or "Did you cost your team the game?" was asked of him, and he responded, to them all. One interviewer asked what it is like having a job in which he is "either the hero or not." Norwood, seeking out no alibi, replied simply, "Well, I realize I let a lot of people down. There is no getting around that."[46] Norwood's accountability and vulnerability under the most dire of circumstances earned him the respect of his teammates and fans, as well as the opposing team, perhaps the ultimate tribute to the power of owning your mistakes.

In Chapter 2, we discussed the *seven deadly sins of speaking* and how they contribute to conflict and communication breakdown. The expert who published that list also developed a converse list of the four best habits of great speakers. He defined them as:

---

[46] See www.youtube.com/watch?v=A6IvwVwkTEo.

"Honesty (be clear and straight),

"Authenticity (be yourself),

"Integrity (be your word),

"Love (wishing people well)."[47]

They are near perfect matches for the concepts of vulnerability that we've been discussing.

Here are examples of vulnerability in action, examples that build trust and strengthen relationships:

- **You let your guard down.** People want to deal with the authentic you, not a false replica. Hollywood stars routinely appear on the late-night circuit to promote a new movie. In most cases, they come across as they do on the big screen, a mere continuation of the characters they play. Ease up, relax, and don't aspire to always be perfect.

- **You can laugh at yourself.** This is the flip side of taking yourself too seriously. You can

---

[47] Julian Treasure, *How to speak so that people want to listen*
See www.youtube.com/watch?v=eIho2S0ZahI&t=19s.

also inject humor, at appropriate times. It breaks up the discussion, lightens tensions, and welcomes the other side to do the same.

- **You aren't Fonzie.** Whether it's saying "I was wrong" or "You were right," say it. I've learned from some of the most seasoned negotiators that a well-timed "Wow, your argument was way better than mine" or "I hate when you are so logical" does more to instill energy in the room than perhaps anything else. You are not going to ingratiate yourself with others by being the unrelenting political talking head that won't give an inch. No one likes the person who is "always right," especially when they're not.

- **You let integrity be your guide.** This may seem like a no-brainer. Of course, we should have integrity. But I am approaching it not just from your own vantage point, but the vantage point of your audience. We'd like to think that the vast majority of us act with personal values that are mostly virtuous. Some reinforce it by talking about it; others just let their actions speak for themselves. The notable point is that you are being observed, and yes, judged by others. How you speak, including to subordinates, how you maintain confidences, how you handle pressure, and what you do to close the deal all leave a trail of behaviors that shape opinions about you.

Anyone with accountabilities feels the strain of pushing through their initiative or plan. While it may be rare for someone to openly cheat, it is not so uncommon to see those motivated by the bottom line to flirt with the edge of the line. Know something when you do it: People are *still* watching you. Put your best foot forward and keep it there. As we discussed in earlier chapters, avoid name-dropping, insults, sharing too much information (whether of the personal or confidential variety), and bending the rules for the sake of getting your way or closing the deal, even when you claim to be doing so in a way that benefits the other side. Even if you are prone to such behaviors or lapses, you should not assume your audience or the opposing side is. Stay clear of it and stand firmly on principles rooted in high character and integrity. Your employees, manager, co-workers, peers, and even those opposing you will respect you for it. And you, in turn, will undoubtedly respect yourself.

When I was a young lawyer, I was on the firm's hiring committee. As such, I was included in the interview loop for every candidate we were looking to hire. Perhaps the most revealing interview was the lunch interview. At ninety minutes, it was longer in length than standard interviews, and allowed you to observe the candidate interact across multiple situations and with various personalities. It also likely revealed a truer picture of the individual, as part of a more casual environment, than what you otherwise would encounter when they were in refined, interview mode.

The discoveries were telling and carried great weight with the rest of the committee. I recall interviewing one candidate over lunch at a nearby hotel restaurant. His credentials were impeccable. He was Ivy-League educated with a track record of achievement and distinction. He passed through the other interviews with flying colors. When I returned from lunch, to the great surprise of the other committee members, I registered a "Do not hire," based on what I observed during our time together. Effectively, this meant we would take a pass on the candidate. The hiring partner dropped by my office after seeing my feedback, which chronicled several instances of our would-be employee expressing impatience and displeasure with the waitress and service. They weren't passing, harmless complaints, but ones that revealed clear traces of harshness and entitlement. When I was done explaining what I saw, the hiring partner said, "You did the right thing. This is *exactly* why we do lunch interviews."

As demonstrated by the Rhode Island justice being swayed by the equities of a case, or Senator Pastore pleasantly succumbing to the emotional appeal of Mr. Rogers, persuasion is a highly relational enterprise. Right or wrong, fair or unfair, people with discretion to embrace what you're selling—or not—will base their decision in no small measure on whether they like and respect the person doing the selling and the manner in which they are selling it.

Express Tips Chapter 5: Be Accountable and Vulnerable

✓ Be accountable.

- Adhere to your *norms of conduct* discussed in Chapter 2.

- Be timely.

- Be responsive.

- Go above and beyond expectations.

- Own up to your mistakes.

✓ Be vulnerable.

- Let your guard down.

- Laugh at yourself, inject humor.

- Don't be Fonzie.

- Always let integrity be your guide.

CONFESSIONS OF A GLOBAL NEGOTIATOR

So, What Do You Do When It Isn't Enough?

OK. You've done everything laid out in this book, but it still wasn't enough. The other side just didn't come around. Maybe they weren't compelled by your vision for success. Or perhaps they just wouldn't budge on your non-negotiables or their must-haves. Now what?

The positive-ending stories I've mentioned didn't end well because they were easy, or somehow lacked the ups and downs or daunting impediments mentioned above. In fact, few did or will. In almost every engagement where give and take is required to advance an idea or to *get a good deal done,* there will be struggles and you will have lapses. Even if you do everything by the book, failures—whether big or small, short-lived or enduring—await you if the other side doesn't reciprocate, or is just plain disagreeable.

The key to dealing with such setbacks? Keep doing what you're doing and continue to live the principles I've discussed. The revelation I hope to leave with you is that by illustrating a compelling vision while eliminating as many obstacles as possible, you dramatically improve your likelihood of success, in persuading others and securing consensus. And the best way of doing so is to focus on that which you control: Your behavior.

Recall in Chapter 3, in the section, "Be constructive. Break the impasse," I said, "It is your job to overcome setbacks and discord. And you deserve little credit until you get there or empty the tank trying." You must persist and persevere. It may well be you face someone on the opposite side who is arrogant, unreliable, and insulting; someone who operates with a very different set of principles: win at all costs, hide the ball, bully and demean, or cut corners or obscure the truth. You likely already have met this person. Their behavior—no matter how distasteful or distrustful—never should serve as an excuse or license for you to lower your own expectations of yourself, in kind. Doing so ensures failure. Worse yet, it compromises your character.

Remain focused on the attributes of persuasion that you control: prepare, paint a picture of success, don't take things personally, be factual, show-don't-tell, be accountable, and maintain your integrity. And return back to them again and again, especially when things get tough. Over time, a positive, constructive, transparent, and accountable approach to communication and problem solving will win out over opposing traits. In most cases, as you persist with consistently positive behaviors, you will find them reciprocated by the other party. At a minimum, they will put you in the very best position for success.

You may be wondering right about now, whatever happened to the "or what" story and how did it end? Well, we closed the deal. But it took three years. The negotiation took every twist and turn you could encounter, with plenty of lapses from my end and considerable demands from the other side. We had our share of clashes. We experienced shifting priorities across our companies, which at one time put all talks on hold for an extended period. And we both defined pictures of success for the deal that changed multiple times during the negotiation. The secret, in the end, was to carry on and remain consistent and predictable in our behaviors. Notwithstanding the occasional turmoil, the commitment each side demonstrated toward a successful conclusion, I believe, left both sides with a feeling of respect and appreciation for the other, and kept the door open to constructive engagements in the future.

Of course, like the Marriott Residence Inn case, not all interactions end on a collaborative note. While much, like your behavior, is within your control, not everything is. Your opposite may demonstrate zero interest in having an aligned viewpoint, on anything. Maintaining reasonableness in your demeanor and position is what's appropriate and expected of you. And you should expect the same of them. You should not read this book to say you may have to accept unreasonable positions, thereby lowering your intended outcomes, or allow yourself to be insulted or bullied just to align with others. You do not.

When I hit a wall in a negotiation, the test I use on myself is as follows: If I was called in to the managing partner's office of my law firm or the CEO's office of my company to explain a lack of progress on a deal worth doing, am I confident they would conclude that I have both:

(a) maintained a principled and reasonable position; and

(b) *emptied my tank*—meaning tried everything within reason—to close the gap with the other side?

If I lack such confidence, I go back to work.

This indeed is a practice I introduced in the three-year negotiated deal mentioned above and in other deals. There are times when despite your best efforts to overcome a significant issue, including your proposing alternative options, your counterpart sometimes just won't give. If it involves a central item and your further compromise on the point would result in a *bad* deal for your company, it may be necessary to call for a regroup along the lines of the following:

> *It appears we've exhausted the options for resolving this issue. I've suggested several ways to fix your concern, all of which you found unacceptable. I believe we've moved past the line of constructive dialogue to solve this and would propose an alternative way forward. Because of the significance of the item we're discussing, I'd like us to each brief our key exec (e.g., CEO/General Counsel)*

on the topic, along with the alternatives we put up, and
have them do a short call and resolve.

Before doing this, be sure that you complete the mental analysis on the above test, and you have concluded the answer to the two questions is *yes* and *yes*. Importantly, be sure your busy exec would agree, as this should be reserved for special cases. What you will find is that this forces the other side to confront the issue in a very similar manner as you and compels them to employ a test not dissimilar to your own. It sharpens focus on both sides, tests the resolve of their entrenched position, and validates their true commitment, or not, in getting the deal done. You will also find that when both sides are forced to work their way through the above test, the discussion usually leads itself back to the negotiating room without the need for executive intervention.

What do you do if they walk away?

If you do deals, it is inevitable that you will experience the other side walking away from the negotiation. What do you do? The first thing is to determine whether it is mere posturing—which it oftentimes is—or is a more genuine reaction to them reaching a walk-away point. Here's what I have learned in these circumstances. Whether you are the one initiating the walk-away, or the other side is, a regroup is the most likely next step, even if it takes a while. Don't overreact. If they walk, I tend to allow time to go by before I even consider initiating contact. This diminishes the appearance of desperation on my part. More importantly, it tests their motivation for walking away. The longer the time lag for them reconnecting, the less likely it was a mere bluff. It also allows the natural flow of backchannel information to gather. If you are working on a complex deal, you likely have multiple connection points with the other side. Use those connections to learn more.

In the end, it may be that giving them anything above their walk-away point simply doesn't measure up for your company. In that case, not doing a deal is the right outcome for you. By the time you reach this point, you will have internally validated and re-validated your own walk-away positions, and will be confident in where you set the line for *getting a good deal done*. You also can be sure that before there is a complete impasse and the deal is declared dead, you—and likely your opponent—will have thought through a form of the above two-part test with your stakeholders. If either side has not yet reached their line, it is more likely than not that you will find yourselves right back at the table, in time.

Concluding Remarks

When I was in law school, I did an internship for the District Attorney's office. In many states, law students who have taken and passed their course on evidence can represent the state or indigent clients in criminal trials. It was a phenomenal experience, as they let me litigate actual cases.

One of my early trials presented a somewhat unusual circumstance. It involved an assault and battery stemming from a fistfight outside of a nightclub. Both parties were arrested at the scene and each pressed charges against the other. This meant there were two sets of prosecutors and defense attorneys involved in the trial. One prosecutor pursued criminal charges against one of the brawlers, with the other prosecutor taking on the other. Each defendant, in turn, was represented by a separate defense attorney.

I got my assignment that morning, and saw that the prosecutor opposite me—i.e., pursuing the criminal claims against my victim and key witness—was my supervisor and lead DA for the district. While we weren't technically on opposite sides, because both of us were representing the state as opposed to either of the defendants, the case was set up for a potential winner or loser.

The lead DA was someone I greatly admired. He was extremely diligent, fair, and committed to justice for the victims of crime. Our trial was reasonably uncomplicated. My supervisor and I both put on our cases, calling witnesses to testify on evidence we hoped would lead to a prosecution. Defense counsel then cross-examined our witnesses and put on evidence of their own to avoid guilty verdicts against their clients. When completed, the judge entered a guilty finding against the defendant I was prosecuting and a not guilty against the defendant my supervisor was prosecuting. This had little, if anything, to do with skill; my side simply had the better facts.

What left an impression on me and that I recall after all these years was what happened later that day. My supervisor took me back to our office and in front of the entire staff, congratulated me on my "victory" at trial. He then spent the afternoon with me talking about the case. He called out the areas where he felt I did well, and the areas where I could have done things differently. He even shared where he felt he messed up. He coached and mentored me, and there wasn't a trace of awkwardness from him in doing so. As I think back on it, I am convinced to this day that he assigned the better side to me, as a way of building up the confidence of this wannabe-lawyer at the start of his career.

Why am I telling this story? As I bring this book to a close, I wanted to leave you with an illustration of someone who embodied so many of the attributes I've discussed in these pages. He prepared and was factual; he personalized, but didn't take things personally; he was accountable; he was vulnerable; he had integrity. He was the model adult at the table that I visualize to this day when I'm dealing with difficult people and complex challenges.

As you start out or look to advance in your career, I'd encourage you to keep your eye out for your own illustrations of people doing things the right way. Ask them questions, seek their mentorship, and try to emulate their positive behaviors. None of us are born with all the skills necessary to be a world-class negotiator or winning advocate. It takes practice and it takes the help of others—others you are likely to find are all too willing to pass on what they have learned during their own pursuit of self-improvement.

In a book I recently read, *The ONE Thing: The Surprisingly Simple Truth Behind Extraordinary Results*, the author aptly captured the essence of such a journey. He said:

> *"When you see someone who has a lot of knowledge, they learned it over time. When you see someone*

who has a lot of skills, they developed them over time. When you see someone who has done a lot, they accomplished it over time . . . The key is over time. Success is built sequentially. It's one thing at a time.[48]

The same is true with negotiating. Hopefully, the lessons I learned and that I've shared with you in this book have given you knowledge, skills, and a big leap forward on your own pursuit of winning advocacy.

---

[48] See *The ONE Thing: The Surprisingly Simple Truth Behind Extraordinary Results* by Gary Keller at (2016) at page 16.

Final Thoughts

When I started this process, as a first-time author, I didn't know what to expect. I had done research many times before: for legal briefs, business plans, presentations, even for the toast as best man at my brother's wedding. This process, however, was different.

Writing this book was a look back not only over my adult life and professional career, but back to my youth. Tapping into the experiences that led to the content for this work allowed me to relive so many incredible memories throughout my life. Even more, it brought back into focus the many friends, colleagues, family members, and even *adversaries* from whom I have learned so much and will forever be grateful to have known. The lessons I learned from each of them, and which I write about, tested me repeatedly during this process. They reminded me that it takes work to persuade and influence with your message; that being an effective storyteller, who is both accountable and vulnerable, is not easy; and that learning to successfully influence and persuade others truly is a process for us all.

From the bottom of my heart, I can only hope that you have enjoyed what I had to share even half as much as I enjoyed sharing it, and importantly, that you will join me in continuing this journey of life-long learning.

Thank you for reading *CONFESSIONS OF A GLOBAL NEGOTIATOR*.

I welcome your direct feedback on the book by sending me email at nickpsy@global-negotiations.com.

If you enjoyed the book, please show your support by providing a review by searching for it by name on www.amazon.com and adding your review where indicated. Reviews are essential for creating visibility for a book and assisting others in their decision to purchase it. Your help here would be greatly appreciated.

Finally, I'd invite you to follow me on LinkedIn and visit my website to stay on top of my latest tips on negotiations:

www.linkedin.com/in/nickpsyhogeos
www.global-negotiations.com

CPSIA information can be obtained
at www.ICGtesting.com
Printed in the USA
FSOW02n1739020417
32550FS